INDIANA OUT LOUD

INDIANA

OUT LOUD

DAN CARPENTER
ON THE
HEARTLAND
BEAT

Indiana Historical Society Press
Indianapolis 2013

Library of Congress Cataloging-in-Publication Data

Carpenter, Dan, 1948-
Indiana out loud : Dan Carpenter on the heartland beat / Dan Carpenter.
    pages cm
ISBN 978-0-87195-308-7 (cloth : alk. paper)
1. Indiana—Social life and customs. I. Title.
F526.6.C373 2013
977.2—dc23
                        2012044318

To Mary

Contents

Preface

In 1993 I published a collection of my writings for the *Indianapolis Star* under the title *Hard Pieces: Dan Carpenter's Indiana*. A kind of double entendre suggested itself, in that the book was presented as a mosaic of jagged fragments from a trying period of recent history, as observed by one who might be familiar to a fair number of readers who had felt the influence of the state's largest newspaper.

The ensuing years have added heavily to this store of personal, engaged journalism; and the sequel to *Hard Pieces* that has been distilled from those hundreds of columns, feature articles, and literary profiles demands a title and central metaphor more dynamic, more disturbing than anything that may have worked before this unforeseeable millennial crossing we have made as members of the regional and global families.

Indiana Out Loud presumes to make itself heard as a distinct voice of this place in this time of economic struggle, political divisiveness, creative persistence, flammable faith, terror brought home, and war, seemingly without end or limit.

The cumulative sound comprises the sweet and strident, the measured and manic, the deafening and the barely detectable. It is as sharp as the orchestrations of a legendary neighborhood grocer and as seductive as the baritone riffs of a celebrated junkie poet. It shrieks against arbitrary war and enforced poverty. It sings the pain of inevitable loss and the praises of improbable gift bearers.

A cacophony, blending into a chorus that packs the urgency of the here and now without losing the beat of our unique history. Can one writer's work capture, possess, and share it even for one enshrining moment? Any claim I might make for that resides in the audience cultivated over more than two decades as a feature writer and "house liberal" editorialist for a publication that boasts of a million Sunday readers but exasperates that large portion of them whose politics place them left of the GOP (and often of the Hoosier Democrats).

My bent for looking at Indiana and the world from odd angles, portraying them with unexpected language and commenting on them from an idealistic and subversive point of view have earned loyalty and enmity in roughly equal volumes, as evidenced by a steady flow of mail from throughout the territory and, thanks to the cosmic reach of the Internet, far beyond. An e-mail from Washington, D.C.; Tel Aviv; or Port-au-Prince has a way of concentrating the mind of the regional writer. It also reminds him of the old Heartland admonition, "Don't get above your raisin'." Alas, I have to say with a shudder—too late.

1

Beneath the Noise

The newspaper columnist who presumes to be the voice of the common man and woman kids himself and cheats his subjects, pardon the ambiguity. He should find it more than challenge enough to serve as ear to the ambient sounds of the city and countryside, and amplifier and interpreter for the often unnoticed, or at least underexamined people, at their source. As the following selections testify, he often becomes their eulogist, holding his homage until their lives' final event.

The voice he gives to their stories must be his own, not speaking for them but taking and giving a reading on them. (Often, he carries a burden of finality—the best character sketches tend to be obituaries.) How does he do justice to a parade that can accommodate a movie strongman turned wrestling impresario, a congresswoman born to an unwed teenager, a middle-aged immigrant radicalized by American labor practices, a subsistence farmer driven to the barricades by rapacious development, an artiste of retailing who became an urban institution? Such a question can go unanswered as long as "Hoosier" defies definition.

Menacker Answers the Bell

JANUARY 18, 1994

He had that showman's tongue-in-cheek integrity, that piquant blend of playfulness and huffy sanctimony that makes a true character.

He never let his guard or his audience down, even if it was an audience of one.

Ask him if wrestling was fake, and he would dial his ringside announcer's nasal New York voice up just a tone or two above the reach of candid conversation and proclaim it a blood sport pure as the first Olympiad.

"But, Sam, how could a guy really get his head pounded six times against a steel ring post and survive, much less jump up mad?"

"That," he replied, "just shows you the incredible conditioning of these athletes."

Sam was a pretty fair athlete himself in his day—a minor league baseball player and a professional wrestler in the sport's long-ago semilegitimate era. He played strongman roles in several movies, his crowning cinematic moment being a defeat in a tug-of-war with a giant ape named *Mighty Joe Young*.

My generation knew him as the impresario and television voice of *Championship Wrestling*, the local grunt-and-growl operation whose threadbare innocence made it more fundamentally entertaining than the intentionally camp Hulk Hogan phenomenon that shoved it aside in the 1980s.

Not that Sam, with his bull neck and his crusher handshake, would just sit and surrender to being the little guy. He talked glory. He was the all-star wrestler; the former husband of June Byers, the all-star lady wrestler; the onetime manager of Gorgeous George Wagner, the archetypal villain wrestler; and partner of the late Dick "Bruiser" Afflis, the World's Most Dangerous Wrestler.

"We made a terrific team," he said of Bruiser and company, who did indeed build something of a national name. "We made history together."

Sam talked big, and people loved him for it. They knew it was shtick and he knew they knew it was shtick; and besides that, everyone knew Sam was no bag of gas.

Besides his considerable accomplishments in the entertainment world, he was a quick-witted and cosmopolitan man who lived, and made a living, just about everywhere.

He was gregarious and courtly in a way that was both Old World and Old Neighborhood. He kissed a woman's hand when he met her. He played card tricks and quoted William Shakespeare. He would slide so neatly from a stage boast to a self-deprecating one-liner; he would have to pause like a Borscht-Belt comedian for the listener to catch up.

"I checked the obituaries myself," he declared in a phone call from El Paso, Texas, back in 1986. "I'm like Mark Twain. The reports are exaggerated."

He was responding to rumors around Indianapolis, his former stomping grounds, that he had died. His barker's voice, even thinned by the miles of sky, put that nonsense to rest.

But he was not the Sam of B movies and step-over toeholds. He was past seventy, was caring for a gravely ill wife (Sandra, his sixth), and was wistful.

"My dad is buried in Indianapolis and I get that feeling once in a while," he said. "I was very close to him."

It was vintage Sam—full of grandiosity, grace and laughter. It would be our last conversation. Slammin' Sammy Menacker died on Janurary 7, seventy-nine years after they broke the mold.

Onliest One Alive
JUNE 15, 1995

Between a picture window shimmering with late-morning sunlight and a neatly made bed decorated with stuffed animals, Hyacinth Thrash slumps in her wheelchair, motionless and silent.

Her thin right fist is tucked under her chin, the arm bent permanently by a spinal injury more than a half-century old, an affliction that also led to the amputation of her left leg.

Her weary eyes stare across the nursing home room toward a cabinet that holds a television, a picture of Jesus Christ, and a new book, of which this ninety-year-old woman is the author.

"Why don't I read Chapter Four to you?" asked Marian Towne, opening the little paperback, getting a flickering of the eyes in response.

And she begins, a white writer and teacher sounding the words of a black survivor of one of history's worst atrocities: "Zip saw him first. She came running in from the other room, shouting, 'I've found my church!' She saw the integrated choir on TV and Jim standing so handsome, and wanted to go."

The lady in the wheelchair has faded a great deal in the last year or so. It is impossible to tell how sharply she still feels her memories of the Reverend Jim Jones and the suicide/massacre of him and nine hundred of his followers at Jonestown, Guyana, in 1978.

Her longest utterance comes in a near-whisper as her collaborator is preparing to leave: "I like to have people come and read."

Towne needs to hear that. Author of two other books, she self published *The Onliest One Alive* after shopping it around to several publishers because she feared she would run out of time to show her friend the fruit of their labor. The book was distilled from sixty hours of interviews over twelve years.

"No part of the Jonestown message was told (before) through the life story of a poor, black, elderly, disabled woman," Towne said. "She alone survived. That says something about her character."

The Onliest One Alive also is the title of a documentary film Towne helped make in the late 1980s about the gallant woman, who used that expression to describe the Sunday morning she woke up surrounded by bodies in a South American jungle.

Though some People's Temple members had escaped by running into the jungle, Thrash was the only survivor on the grounds when rescuers arrived. Her sister and lifelong companion, Zipporah, was among the dead.

Towne and Thrash met through Catherine Wallace, a grand-niece of

Thrash who attends Towne's church. As it happened, Towne also had an acquaintance who died at Jonestown.

Feeling enough had been written about Jones, the Indianapolis civil rights activist turned cult tyrant, Towne decided to emphasize the survivor's path to Jonestown—from rural childhood in Jim Crow's Alabama to "colored jobs" in politely segregated Indianapolis to "heaven on Earth" in California, the destination of the People's Temple's first exodus.

Thrash, who felt from childhood she had the divine gift of healing, joined Jones's flock because the white preacher fought for racial equality and because, she believes, he cured her of breast cancer.

Eventually, Jones's obsessions with sex, money, and power would alienate her. She began to doubt him when she spoke with him about adopting a child, and he replied that she couldn't get a white one: "You can tell a lot about a person by a slip of the tongue. I should have left the church right there."

Instead, she stayed and followed, to the West Coast and abroad. She did not want Zip to go without her. She was divorced, had no children, and was unable to work because a poorly treated injury from her younger days had progressed too far. Jones promised her a job and the opportunity to use her healing powers: "We were brainwashed! Programmed, like with dope!"

Towne surmises that Thrash's disability and age made her insignificant to Jones and his guards and enabled her to hide undetected under a bed on November 18, 1978, while the rest were assembled for death, either by drinking cyanide-laced Flavor-Aid or by being shot: "I remember those babies marching past our place with little paper hats on, wearing sandals, sunsuits and matching shorts and tops. It's enough to make you scream your lungs out, thinking of those babies dead."

In addition to telling the story of one historic life, Towne hopes the book sounds an alarm about self-anointed messiahs such as Jones and David Koresh, who supplant their followers' families and stockpile guns.

"There's a tension in our culture," Towne said. "We do respect people's right to choose their own faith. But the press and the news media have a responsibility to show the truth."

Towne suggests the media could have discredited Jones before he took his church to California in 1965. She also wonders whether a better racial climate in Indianapolis would have lessened his appeal to blacks, who were tired of the bigotry that whites would not acknowledge.

The Onliest One Alive lays down Thrash's burden starting with the byline on the cover: "Catherine (Hyacinth) Thrash." She legally changed her name to Catherine as a young woman and yet remains known by the name given her in childhood by a white woman for whom her mother worked.

"I'll leave it right here, Hyacinth," Towne said, putting the book on the shelf next to the television, "so you can have someone read it to you whenever you want."

She hugs the author and leaves her to rest: "I don't hold a grudge 'bout color, if folks treat me right. Blacks are not ones to hold a grudge."

Postscript
NOVEMBER 29, 1995

Once in a while we are reminded how short this nation's history is, how much of its share of the line of human progress can be segmented in a single life.

Catherine Hyacinth Thrash was born long enough ago to have known slaves, and lived long enough to see a black conservative named to the Supreme Court.

She was part of the northward exodus from Jim Crow, part of a generation of proud domestic workers who made their prickly peace with segregation, and part of a rural religious tradition that believed in shouting preachers and healing hands and praying for one's enemies.

I daresay she underestimated her own magnanimity and serenity when she said, in the paperback memoir published a few months before her death, "I don't hold a grudge 'bout color, if folks treat me right."

In a life that ended on November 18 after ninety-three years, Thrash endured wrong treatment of criminal, even historic, enormity; and yet she offered little evidence she held a grudge against even the worst of the perpetrators.

As a girl in the fondly remembered Deep South, she inherited racially prescribed boundaries to her education and future.

As a young woman, she was crippled for life when she fell from a moving truck and was not properly doctored.

As a pensioner seeking companionship and a way to express her Christian faith, she was lied to, stolen from, and nearly slaughtered by a self-anointed messiah named Jim Jones.

Thrash is a historical footnote, the sole survivor found in the People's Temple compound in Jonestown, Guyana, after Jones's orgy of cyanide Flavor-Aid and gunfire killed nine hundred men, women, and children in 1978.

"The onliest one alive" was her plaintive proclamation; a phrase that became the title of a documentary film about her ordeal and of the book a writer friend, Marian Towne, helped her assemble. It was a joy to Towne that she was able to present the finished book to its author and read it to her at the nursing home where she spent her last months.

When Towne called me on the morning of Hyacinth's death, she said she was certain, despite the mental drifting toward the end, that her friend had been aware and happy her story was in print. For a woman who may have owed her life to anonymity (Jones's henchmen never bothered to check under her bed as they swept the compound), the little book with her picture on the cover and her lost country language preserved on its pages was a triumph.

Perhaps her age and infirmity had caused her to be overlooked by the guards; but her mind and will already had separated her from the false prophet, and she later said she heard God telling her she was being spared because she had done right. She who had humbled herself was exalted.

"No part of the Jonestown message was told (before) through the life story of a poor, black, elderly, disabled woman," Towne said last summer after my final visit with Thrash. "She alone survived. That says something about her character."

Her survival, not just in Guyana but in Alabama and in Indianapolis, speaks to a nation's character. Her life was an allegory about racism, demagoguery, and the sovereignty of persons. While we were listening to all sorts of noise, she was telling our story.

School Day in the Life

FEBRUARY 26, 1995

At 6:30 a.m. on a winter Tuesday, Dick Pritchard is taking on a light load of fuel for a long trip.

Dressed for work in his trademark suspenders and pop-art necktie, he hunches over a bowl of cereal at the kitchen counter and talks a little shop and a little household business with his wife, Deborah, who's starting her day with a cup of tea.

Visible through the back window are the lights of North Central High School on Eighty-sixth Street, where Pritchard will drop off his sons, Brian, a junior, and Rob, a freshman, on his way to Allisonville Elementary School on Seventy-ninth Street.

As 7 a.m. approaches and passes, the boys trudge downstairs, take their turns in the cereal rotation at the counter, then pile into their father's well-traveled Oldsmobile.

He grabs his briefcase, kisses his wife, and charges into a day that will not end until the paper grading is done at 9:15 p.m., or so.

At age forty-five, after twenty-two years of teaching, "he still likes it," said Deborah, a preschool teacher herself. "Once in a while he talks of changing his situation, but something or someone always comes along to keep him interested."

One of those things is technology; another is the volunteer help Pritchard has been getting from several dads in his coaching of wrestling.

Partial to math and science, he pushes the use of computers in his fifth-grade classroom and is on a technology committee for Washington Township Schools. He will spend most of his brief lunch period today instructing some fourth graders in computer use.

A wrestling meet at Northview Middle School will occupy him from immediately after school until about 7:30 p.m., suppertime at last. It's one of three sports that Pritchard coaches for extra pay during the school year.

His team will lose the dual meet by forfeiting the final match when Pritchard refuses to let his guy wrestle a girl. "There's no way I can rationalize that," he said, referring to a phenomenon that's caused other standoffs in the Indianapolis area. In terms of emotion and voice volume, Deborah observed, "you see an entirely different person" when Pritchard leaves the elementary classroom to work with middle-school athletes.

Not that Room 3 at Allisonville does not generate intensity of its own.

This morning, Steve Chaney will set Pritchard off by announcing during one of the math group sessions that an older boy, not part of the school, has bullied him once again, this time by stealing his binder full of homework.

"I'm not mad at you, I'm mad at him," Pritchard snapped, jabbing his finger toward the diminutive blond kid. "If you won't tell him, I will. . . . He's not going to mess with your education. If he does, he'll have to go through me."

Displeasure of a milder variety erupts at recess time, when a district policy is invoked that requires pupils to be indoors during extreme cold. Disdainful of the rule, Pritchard tells his moaning and groaning class, "Don't complain to me; complain to the superintendent." As Pritchard plays chess with some of the imprisoned pupils, others pass a mock petition.

Before recess comes lunch, which is supposed to be at 11:40 a.m. but might be 11:45 a.m. or so, depending on whether Pritchard is on a pedagogical roll. His mornings take up the bulk of the day's instructional time, and he packs them. Today is no exception.

Early on, there's poetry. Formula poems such as haikus and cinquains. Free-form poems for the free-spirited.

"Don't say to me, 'I can't write poetry,'" Pritchard exhorted. "Anyone can write poetry."

On to science, which today involves the effects of adding and subtracting energy. Boiling and freezing water, for example. Contrary to what's widely believed, Pritchard says, water does not expand when it freezes, it contracts. He draws the H-O-H molecule to show the bonds that shrink with cold.

"I know what you're going to ask me. Go ahead."

"I put my dad's beer in the freezer, and it kind of exploded."

"We're dealing with lots of variables here. It's a pressurized container, for one thing."

Attention turns to the early American colonies, subject of an upcoming essay test. Pritchard writes "Mayflower Compact" on the clear plastic easel of the overhead projector, then adds "equal laws—all people."

He takes a long pause.

"I'm going to be a little bit wrong here. Did they really care about all people?"

The class understands. Issues of race and gender are not new to this room.

"The Equal Rights Amendment would have had no chance. They were talking about adult males," Pritchard said. But the concepts of self-government and religious freedom, he goes on to point out, were of historic magnitude nonetheless.

Math groups take the class up to lunchtime and continue after lunch and recess.

The last forty-five minutes of the day, up to dismissal at 2:20 p.m., are taken up by Project DARE, in which a police officer talks to the class about drugs while the teacher catches up on paperwork.

Pritchard can use the time. He endorses the idea of helping kids say no to negative influences. But he's never content having someone else running his classroom.

Having arrived about 7:30 a.m., a half hour before his class, Pritchard will leave for his wrestling meet after seven hours in the building. Nearly that many more hours will elapse before the workday ends.

Most of those additional hours will be spent in virtually constant motion—dragging mats into place, mopping them with disinfectant, setting up the scoreboard, pacing the sidelines, yelling, congratulating, and consoling.

"When teaching or coaching reach the point where they're not fun anymore, I'll be gone," he said. "I hope that's not for a long time."

Land of Plenty
SEPTEMBER 16, 1996

One of the happiest single moments I've spent as a newspaper writer was a bright, muddy fall afternoon in 1988 at Bob Klawitter's little farmstead outside of Dubois, near Patoka Lake.

It was lambing time, and big Bob and I took turns cuddling the precious pink-and-white critters as he explained how he had gone through the difficult process of learning how to kill them.

I was deep into the writings of Wendell Berry and other defenders of agrarian tradition back then, as indeed I still am, and I lapped up the mixture of loveliness, serenity, and tragedy that the rural way of life gave and demanded. To turn all five senses loose on it on a fine crisp day, on company time, was like stealing for a living.

Klawitter could empathize. This was no more second nature to him than it was to me. A city boy most of his life, a college professor when he had last held an official job, Klawitter had moved to the hills with the intention not of retiring or retreating but of being fully there. Studying from books, from his mistakes, and from his neighbors, he would dig, raise, harvest, slaughter, and provide as best he could in his piece of that dwindling wooded country.

He did not try to kid anybody. Money was still required, and his wife, Kathy, supplied that as a schoolteacher. Their son, Sam, liked computers, and so did Klawitter, who rigged up a solar generator for their PC.

Klawitter was not a dreamy primitive or a hermit; he knew how to socialize and how to laugh. But he was in southern Indiana in pursuit of the American dream of being left alone. That simple wish was denied him.

Every morning he spent weeding his tomatoes, the government was busy selling timber from the fragile, fragmented Hoosier National Forest, an essential part of his chosen community.

Every afternoon he whiled away in conversation with old Banks McBride down the road, developers were enlisting investors and politicians for a monstrous theme park on Patoka Lake.

Every evening he sat sipping wine and watching stars from the porch of his homemade house, somebody was trying to resurrect the boondoggle of an interstate highway that would slash Orange County on its way from nowhere to nowhere.

So Klawitter, the weary 1960s activist, found himself strapping on the gun belt again. He fired up his solar computer, revved up his creaky Jeep Cherokee, buttoned up his lumberjack shirts, and made the rounds of letters to the government, letters to the editor, newsletters, news releases, meetings, meetings, and meetings. He once sent me a thirty-five-page fax, a record I hope never falls.

Because he outworked and outthought everyone around him, because he could talk as plain or fancy as the occasion required, and because he refused to treat political opponents as personal enemies, Klawitter won people over and won many battles.

But the war on what is valuable never stops, to paraphrase Berry, so Klawitter could not stop. He was on his way to another battlefront, to a meeting about setting up an environmental protection fund, when he was killed in a car accident a few days ago.

"It's difficult. I resent it," he told me in 1991. "You're always on a wartime basis. Your garden gets run down because you're always being attacked. This is the good life. I wish a lot of people would go away and leave us alone so we can grow our vegetables and cut our firewood."

Like many remarkable people I've met in this line of work, Klawitter was one I wish I had gotten to know better. But in an important social sense, we were too much in touch, too much in the mass marketplace together, too much away from our own gardens. That's the lesson I read in those books, but really took to heart from the example of this good man.

Lord of the Corner

MARCH 26, 1997

Snookie Hendricks was not exactly easy to know, but he was about the easiest guy in town to find.

Over the final few years of his peripatetic and perilous life, the man with the goatee and the little pillbox cap patrolled the corner of Fortieth Street and Boulevard Place so faithfully that I would have been willing to make you a bet: Go and stand there, any time, night or day, and Snookie would materialize inside of fifteen minutes.

It never failed for me; but then, I would not want to pass myself off as an expert on that neighborhood, even if I do live within walking distance of it. Charles "Snookie" Hendricks was an interview subject, feature story material, and nobody knew better than he how little the press knows about the street.

Snookie was a man of the street, a mover and a maker, a face to facer, a politician without pinstripes, a jaybird of alertness, a poet of the hurried conversation, and a hustler in all senses of the word. In his heyday, before "rap" became a term for a specific brand of commercial music, we would have said of him, with a mix of admiration and leeriness, "The cat can rap."

Snookie was, above all, a survivor—a survivor who died, shot in the back March 19 at Fortieth and Boulevard. He was sixty-five years old.

Snookie? Sixty-five? Violent death is never timely and always to be mourned, but it still is strange to think of the eternal brother man at such a milestone.

He made his reputation at a time when youth was being served as never before or since. In the 1960s, university presidents had to negotiate with students who took over their offices, and nervous mayors had to strike truces with a new breed of activist in the rumbling ghettos.

Snookie was the main militant, and the go-between whom Mister Charley presumably needed to see to keep the lid on. He also was rumored to be a police informer, a label he vehemently disputed. The heroin, though, was no rumor; he served prison time for it and said, late in life, that he finally licked it through conversion to Islam.

Many years after he ceased to be the go-to guy, and after City Hall pretty much lost interest in that for which it once went to him, Snookie patrolled the sidewalk, his gold key to the city pinned to his hat.

When I last talked to him at length, several years ago, he was still rapping about starting a youth center, still rapping about how old men in the neighborhood did not know how to talk to kids. But he, too, feared the new generation a little. In front of his sharp eyes, the communal fire of the Panthers and Pan-Africanists that once commanded America's attention had gone deadly cold. Revolution, real or romantic, had degenerated into dog-eat-dog. Young blacks were turning on each other, and one of those young people, police say, killed Snookie.

His legacy, like his life, is full of ambiguity and contradiction. With Snookie, you can take your pick. I prefer to remember him for his stubborn belief that older people are the trouble when young people make trouble.

In front of Snookie's eyes at Fortieth and Boulevard, a white artist named Carol Tharp-Perrin helped a bunch of teenagers paint a giant sky-blue mural on the side of a brick building. Graced with images of Frederick Douglass, Malcolm X, Reverend Martin Luther King Jr., John F. Kennedy, and other reformers of history, it remains, after five years, unsullied by graffiti. I drive by and remind myself not to be surprised by that. I ought to know by now that even in the most desperate of times, there is a spirit that keeps its feet, keeps talking, and keeps hustling, refusing to die.

Maestro of Margin
SEPTEMBER 8, 2000

It was years before I learned Sid Maurer's last name, and it was not until I read it in his obituary that I finally committed it to memory.

I hope I have done so, anyway. Formal things matter when someone important becomes history, a permanent and ever-present loss that we are obliged to appreciate in full.

Sid, in life, to the countless north siders like myself who knew him on business, was just Sid. A dignified, even a patriarchal figure, to be sure, surveying the aisles from his little conning tower next to the checkout lanes, solemnly greeting each customer as if that person's arrival made a quorum. But never a Mister, except to the generations of high school kids who stuffed bags under his supervision.

Business was personal at Atlas Supermarket, where the volume of goods per square foot defied physics and a jam-packed crowd flowed like a minuet and nobody waiting at the deli took a number.

"This is a *community*," a friend of mine proclaimed one Saturday as we maneuvered through capacity cart traffic in zero space with no rancor. It was one of the few times the sound of that overused word has had any ring to it for me.

When Sid started working in his father-in-law's store fifty-three years ago, the neighborhood grocery was where the weekly shopping still got done in America. Gigantism was slouching toward us in our hubris of military victory, but small still had some beauty. Coca-Cola did not come in cases of twenty-four and superstores with ATMs out on the prairie were unfathomable.

Sid had himself a good neighborhood, an elite neighborhood, as he bought into the business and set sail with his fellow independent grocers on the wide, calm seas of post-World War II prosperity. A couple decades later, he was out there virtually by himself. A full-fledged supermarket that also handles gourmet food, plus kosher, plus a steam table with twenty-five-cent hot dogs, plus floral bouquets and recipe advice and wines personally guaranteed by the proprietor—how do you pull that off in the shadow of Cub?

Though the store, for reasons forever to be speculated upon, did not survive his passing, Sid would be the first to tell you he had good help in his success, from his bride, Eleanor, and niece, Debbie, through a bunch of other veterans who seemed capable of running a Cub but happy to be at Fifty-fourth Street and College Avenue. The high school sackers may have had varying degrees of allegiance, but they boasted the legacy of David Letterman, who still cherishes his experience as a sack boy and apprentice comedian under Sid's merciful glare.

If Atlas was more than Sid, though, it was inseparable from him, as he was from it. There is a genius to the daily negotiation of perishable food that I cannot begin to understand, but I certainly get the "daily" part of it. When you run a restaurant or grocery, you've got to be there; or at least you feel you have to, which amounts to the same thing.

I cannot estimate the number of trips I've made to Atlas, but I feel certain I can count on my fingers the times I did not see Sid there. Atlas may have distinguished itself by being closed Sundays, but I daresay nobody at the 24-7 stores is aiming to put in a half century of six-day weeks.

Peering over his glasses, proper in his necktie, Sid was equally ready to help me find a four-dollar bottle of wine and to welcome a lady who had stepped out of a Rolls-Royce into the store she had shopped in when it was new.

Like any artist, he labored for our pleasure. Like so many of his generation, he labored in retailing so that his children would have a choice between the family business and the professions. The history of produce and groceries in Indianapolis is a saga of Italian and Jewish progress and assimilation in which the Jewish owner of Atlas Supermarket is one of the heroes.

Though their clientele were worlds apart, Atlas always reminded me of Stein's Ideal Market off Fountain Square, where our family bought on credit when I was a child. Max Stein made more than a fair living off a poor neighborhood far from the one he resided in; but when my mother's final illness was eating up our money, he sort of forgot about our tab.

It is inevitable, we are told, that the stories end and the ethnic groups scatter and city lovers get left with distant megamalls where nobody slows our commerce with conversation. Sid, whose funeral burst the capacious confines of Congregation Beth-El Zedeck, was proof it does not have to happen. Even if it only briefly outlived him, Atlas likewise was proof, an ever-moving monument, in its allotted time, to a man's faith.

Julia, Bill, and the Color of Dreams
OCTOBER 27, 2000

Once you've subtracted the Republicans, the scolds, and the people who have just plain seen too much politics, you are left with less than a majority who can get misty-eyed over the moment Julia Carson enjoyed on a fall weekend in Indianapolis at the millennial turn.

The black daughter of a single mother, a generation removed from going to work every morning in a white uniform, stood at a podium and heard the president of the United States, Bill Clinton, praise her name and lend his powerful support to her re-election to Congress.

It was not Frank Capra melodrama, to be sure. It was a professional show by veteran politicians with connections to various interests that may or may not serve your interests. The whole affair was sniped at by Carson's enemies, and Clinton's, which is as it should be in an open society with issues.

But still.

Is there anyone with soul so dead as to not at least nod when this child of poverty and segregation exults that she has stepped beyond her dreams?

Did you yourself not imagine, way back before there were presidents you approved of and presidents you did not, what it would be like to know the occupant of the White House personally?

Can you picture yourself imagining such an attainment when you're a kid in Indianapolis at mid-century, politely barred from certain amusement parks and swim clubs because of your skin?

Yes, they had a dream. But it took a large soul to dream just of equality; to dream of being the one who takes a whole city's aspirations to Washington would have been a masterpiece of the mind.

Today, the reality of a black female congressperson from conservative Indianapolis (not to mention a black Republican challenger; we won't cheat you, Marvin Scott) is pretty much routine—until an occasion comes to remind everyone we are living through history.

For all the baggage he may carry, Clinton is a courier of joy to people such as Carson and her supporters, black and white. Not only does he represent the only major political party minorities and the poor can call home, he himself has seen some trouble and kept his eye on the prize.

At a time when both of the viable candidates for president are wealthy sons of Washington politicians, Clinton, whatever one thinks of his policies or his principles, proves that a kid from a broken home in a forgotten state can succeed in the face of powerful and ruthless white opposition.

It is not as if fatherlessness is an accepted African American trait; but it is one of many disadvantages to which people on the margins of society can relate.

The eminent black author Toni Morrison caused a justified stir when she wrote in *The New Yorker* that Clinton was "blacker than any actual person who could be elected in our children's lifetime," then went on to explain she was referring to single motherhood, poverty, saxophone playing, and eating at McDonald's.

Nasty stereotypes? Well, she was overly cryptic at the very least. But ask people in the inner city if they would root for a guy with those characteristics against a politician who does not know the retail price of a gallon of milk, and guess what you'll get.

You will get the kind of acclamation we witnessed at the Indiana State Fairgrounds, when Clinton and Carson stood together at a pinnacle that America at last has made reachable from the ground and not just the foothills.

This history we've seen made is not ancient. It took interminable lawsuits, hard-fought legislation, strife on the streets, and violent death, and most of that took place within a contemporary congresswoman's lifetime.

Race, poverty, and expansion of opportunity are not prominent issues in the current political campaigns. Those who have begrudged Clinton his key to the White House—columnist George Will, voice of the blue-suit Republicans, calls the president and his wife "vulgarians"—may well elect his replacement. They have tried to show, with their clumsy display of tokens of color, that they are ready to embrace the reality of America. What they cannot grasp is the dream.

Middle East Meets Middle West
SEPTEMBER 14, 2001

He fled to America from a place where foreign soldiers roamed the streets, where they took the liberty of barging into his home to make sure his family was behaving.

Three decades later, he has come about as far as one can travel in the fond but futile pursuit of a life free of strife.

This week, he was reminded, with apocalyptic force, that there is no refuge.

"It is a tragic, tragic event," Mina Khoury said. "It hits so close to home. We run away to a country where we can find peace, and it hits us. This will change the way we all live."

Khoury is not naive and never has sought insulation. Many times, he has visited his original home of Bethlehem, which he and his mother and two siblings left in 1968 out of weariness from the Israeli military occupation that ensued from the 1967 war. Constantly, in local community meetings and letters to the editor, he has spoken out for a Middle East rapprochement that recognizes the rights of his kindred Palestinians. He has felt the slings of those who equate criticism of Israel with anti-Semitism, and those who equate Palestinians with terrorists, and those who assume Palestinian reaction to mass murder is typified by a cheering crowd on television.

Yet Khoury is hardly a firebrand or a cosmopolitan snob. He runs an ice-cream parlor in the affluent suburb where he resides with his wife, Eloisa, and teenage son, Alexander. "Love it or leave it," that ugly argument-stopper from the 1960s that's sure to resurface in these times, does not apply. Prejudice, he says, has not been a problem.

"We've found it quite easy. Indiana is home to us," he said. "Whenever I go somewhere else, I feel as if I ought to be back here."

Night after night this week, Khoury has been at Saint George Orthodox Christian Church for services mourning the thousands of victims and beseeching comfort for their families.

"We are utterly disgusted by this tragic incident," he said. "It is not just an act of terror against the United States but against the cause of peace itself."

In his native land, where open hostility and lethal conflagrations have held sway for nearly a year, progress toward the peace that leaders have mapped out in boardrooms will be set back even further, he fears. Americans and Israelis will be hardened in their mentality of Arab collective guilt.

Whoever committed this atrocity, Khoury declared, "does not portray the feelings of Arabs, of Palestinians."

And yet, there was that jubilation when his adopted country was at its nadir.

Slowly, deliberately, he addressed that painful scenario, asking not acceptance but awareness. "In the West Bank, in Lebanon, in the refugee camps, what you're seeing comes out of frustration with what has happened in the last ten months," said Khoury.

Curfews, sweep arrests, roadblocks that thwart getting to work and to the grocery, the commandeering and destruction of homes, and shooting and shelling, all in the name of security; certainly a critical Israeli concern. But all directed against Palestinians, who are expected to submit to military rule not because of what they do but because of who they are.

Khoury remembers. He was fourteen when his family left it behind. "I had never seen soldiers with guns before. They intimidated us in every aspect of our lives," he remembered. "They imposed curfews. They came into our home many times, at night and in the middle of the day, supposedly searching for weapons. Three teenagers and a widow. Obviously, they were targeting people who could be intimidated, so they would be compelled to leave. We were among the lucky ones. We found peace and tranquility in the United States."

Now, he grieves for his fellow Americans. He prays for a U.S. government that he believes has greater influence for mideastern peace than it has exerted. He prays as a Christian to the God of Muslims and Jews. "Our religions teach us to love one another," he said, "not to fight and kill one another."

Sy Rowe, on the Case
DECEMBER 12, 2001

Who could have imagined it a few years earlier?

A bus parked at the corner of Twenty-eighth and Olney Streets, taking on black teenagers for a trip to a dance—at Perry Meridian High School on the far south side.

A federal court order, fought by suburbanites and their lawyers for more than a decade, had made the inner-city youths Perry Meridian Falcons.

A school and its parents, white and black, had decided that the bused students, regardless of the circumstances under which they came, must be full-fledged students. This meant, among many other measures, after-hours transportation to school events.

It also meant the hiring of home-school advisers such as Sylvester Rowe.

A black minister with lengthy experience as a professional equal opportunity officer, Rowe knew the goodwill between the communities was a precious and threatened sapling. He had seen how rock throwing and Ku Klux Klan graffiti made headlines and gave comfort to those who did not want to see desegregation work. He had been in the South in the 1960s, and he felt the pressure history once again was imposing upon young African Americans.

That night in 1986 he was looking for black kids to exclude.

Nothing personal. He just wanted the neighborhood guys who did not attend Perry Meridian, and proposed to worm their way onto the bus for who-knows-what purpose, to go make their own action and leave his bunch alone.

Rowe suffered cuts on the mouth and head, damage to his inner ear, and injuries to his knees so severe he eventually had to have them both replaced.

When I met him a few years later, he was walking with laborious effort, sometimes with canes. He had given his hide to human progress, to young people, and the only pride he displayed was in them and in the communities they bridged.

He would escort me through the sprawling school, introducing me to this black honor student or that black football player or homecoming queen. He would find himself greeting more white students than black. He did not indulge in a lot of avuncular sentimentality about racial harmony.

"You will be accepted," he said, "when people see you can do something. Sports, art, music—a talent. That's the key: what you do."

Still, integration did not come easy. Even the athletes, whose talent and value were the most obvious, faced the logistical monster of making it back and forth for practices and games. Under the leadership of Rowe and others, such as then-Perry Meridian principal James Head, Perry Township became the first of the districts receiving bused students from

Indianapolis Public Schools to offer transportation for extracurricular activities.

As Rowe readily pointed out, many families in Perry Township threw their homes open to bused kids after school on event nights, and many put their own cars into service when buses were not available. Rowe drove his own car, and his body, into the ground.

Trips to the neighborhoods were eye-openers. Some areas were not pretty; some were not safe. Rowe knew this long before some hoodlums demonstrated it to him. He considered himself fortunate. He knew kids from the bused area who had been taken by the street.

"Sometimes you wonder why you just don't give up," he told me in 1991. "I've been to too many funerals."

He soldiered on until 1993 as Perry Meridian's home-school adviser. He died at age seventy this past December 1, having seen more than his share of lives lost and lives launched.

"We had a very positive, close working relationship," Head recalls. "It was Sy's idea that parents of the bused kids, not just the kids, needed to be involved. He was a problem solver. And he had high expectations for the kids."

There's really no measuring his legacy. It is one with school desegregation itself, an accomplishment that it has become fashionable to disparage or even dismiss.

In Indianapolis today, unlike in my school days, miles apart does not mean worlds apart. We tend to forget how significant that is, and we have scant appreciation for the sacrifices our limited progress has exacted. It would help us, I think, if we carried a mental picture of a school bus that included a good man, working late, guarding its doors.

Nowhere Better
SEPTEMBER 28, 2003

Bean Blossom, IN—The hills and hollers, woods and pastures of this fifty-five acre patch of pickers' paradise were carpeted with humanity, motor vehicles, and temporary shelters by last Wednesday, eve of a world-famous bluegrass festival that ends this weekend.

But on a sunny Tuesday morning around a sputtering campfire behind concession row, a handful of men who know every oak and gravel chunk had Bill Monroe's Memorial Music Park and Campground just about to themselves.

There was B. C. "Lightning" Hannemann, crowned "King of the Hippies" by the late Mr. Bill himself. And Chubby Dickens, who used to drive the bus for the great Jimmy Martin and thinks he might be kin to Little Jimmie Dickens of Opry immortality.

And W. M. Bentley, around so long his campsite is officially named for him, as is a hiking path around the grounds.

And the elder statesman, Jim "Colonel" Peva, a retired Indiana State Police officer and Indiana University professor who has this place in perspective as perhaps nobody else has.

Peva's been a regular since 1961, when he brought his wife, Ailene, and three young daughters for a first taste of the elixir that made Monroe, father of Bluegrass, an American legend.

"When that fiddle started in on 'Watermelon Hangin' on a Vine,' the hair stood up on the back of my neck," the soft-spoken gent recalled with a rhapsodic smile. "Somewhere in my ancestral genes there had to be a connection."

The Monroe and Peva families grew close over the years, with Jim evolving into an unpaid jack-of-all-trades for the operation as well as its historian. The map of this Brown County landmark lists his camping spot, Peva's Place, right along with Bentley's. The most impressive structure on the grounds, the Bluegrass Hall of Fame and Country Star Museum, includes, in its trove of effects from the likes of Roy Acuff and Johnny Cash, various photographs taken by Peva and a framed copy of a lifetime pass Monroe presented to the family after Jim ran the show during an emergency in 1977.

The seventy-five-year-old Plainfield resident is working with a University of Kentucky professor to get the site, home of string music festivals for more than sixty years running, listed on the National Register of Historic Places. He's also campaigning for a commemorative postage stamp for the namesake, who died in 1996 and will be eligible in 2006. A recent petition collected signatures around the grounds from thirty-five states and six foreign countries, and they missed the Japanese campers.

Some 20,000 lovers of bluegrass were expected for Uncle Pen Days, the four-day jamboree that ends this evening. Named for the relative who raised an orphaned Monroe and taught him music, the event is both old as the hills and young as the spirit of Dwight Dillman, an entrepreneur from Miami County who played banjo with Monroe's Bluegrass Boys in 1974 and returned two decades later to save the place from being sold for a housing development. Dillman has poured money into it and has events running from mid-May to mid-October. He's not much for tooting his own horn, if you'll pardon the mismatched metaphor; but Peva will do it for him, and for the honest American culture that abides here.

"It's just a beautiful place," Peva said, surveying the summery greenscape rolling down toward a porch-sized stage where early arrivals had staked out their lawn chairs. "I wanted to spend my retirement with bluegrass and genealogy. I can't imagine anywhere better."

Doc, Ray, Gains, Losses
JANUARY 7, 2004

James Counsilman started his long and legendary career as Indiana University men's swim coach at about the same time Ray Crowe started making history at Crispus Attucks High School.

Both were intimately acquainted with history, as in the two defining events of their generation—World War II and the battle over racial injustice. Counsilman's career as a competitive swimmer had been interrupted by service as a bomber pilot. Crowe's workplace was a Jim Crow school, founded in the Ku Klux Klan-influenced 1920s as the venue for blacks who wished to better themselves beyond eighth grade and for those who would teach them.

Could either man have dreamed, in those prim and provincial 1950s, what a grand and gross spectacle his sport would grow to be? Would either of them, presiding with his whistle over a handful of wet faces in an echoing cavern of a practice site, have chosen the precipitous path of glamour and greed that athletics would take in the decades before their deaths?

"Doc" Counsilman, the physiology PhD and scientific tinkerer, was incubating a global phenomenon-to-be in the 1960s and 1970s, when his IU teams dominated swimming and raised its profile. The stars of those pioneering days did not have the competition or the mass-media allure to take over their lives from the preteens, as today's swimmers and divers do. Nor did they have to line up for drug tests.

Crowe's lads, the first all-black team and first Indianapolis team to win the state high school basketball championship, labored without a home fieldhouse and had to hear the city fathers express fear about letting them have a victory parade through downtown. Tigers fans believed (even if white folks swore the opposite) that the referees looked for ways to make them lose. Their dapper, stoical coach, like a mother duck in a minefield, played the hand he was dealt and got his charges through life in segregated Indiana. He lived to see national television pursue a black high school basketball player named LeBron James, informing us breathlessly of his $90 million shoe contract, inviting him to expound on his own greatness as few but Cassius Clay dared in the Attucks heyday.

So much more and so much less. More money, more opportunity, more peril, and less modesty, less patience, and less proportion. No right-thinking person would want young Chinese swimmers or black basketball enthusiasts to live in the world Counsilman and Crowe inherited. But we know the timeless quality of these men's demeanor and devotion, and we feel their loss even as we realize they fit a time that's well done with. We only wish they still fit.

The world that Counsilman left on January 4, at age eighty-three, and Crowe departed December 20, at eighty-eight, has its gentlemen— and women—of sport. But if a Tony Dungy proves that quiet dignity can succeed in a jungle of arrogance, bombast and avarice, he has little chance of becoming typical.

For some of us, Crowe's fleeting appearance as the coach of the losing state finals team was one of the most poignant elements of the movie *Hoosiers*. Truth is, he and Oscar Robertson, et al., wrote a much more significant story than Bobby Plump and Milan High, the film's inspiration. Milan's was the swan song; Attucks blew the trumpet of the future. Had they been able to see it back then, what would the great, modest history makers have made of it all?

The Essential Joe Farah

OCTOBER 16, 2005

For many of those conscientious citizens who give their lives or their weekends over to wildlife, clean water, peace, and justice, the worst fear isn't losing, it's being wrong.

Nobody wins an endless struggle, but the prize can go dim sometimes. You listen to the war makers espouse liberation and the conglomerates tout their community spirit, and you might wonder if they do not own the truth along with everything else.

It is at such moments that you need a Joe Farah.

The bright, civilized scores of friends and admirers who packed his memorial service at Butler University's Robertson Hall last Sunday, marking his death on September 14, heard a litany of virtues that would have sounded like ritual excess to a stranger.

Courage. Integrity. Humility. Compassion. Loyalty. Love.

A Renaissance man. A proud veteran. A visionary.

Bubbling with enthusiasm over a new idea. Seething with anger over lies that kill. Sickly for the last twenty of his sixty-three years, yet getting himself to the keyboard, podium, and picket line even when his body said no.

All true, and all fortifying for that caste of environmentalists, peace activists, campaign finance reformists, corporate critics, and kindred Heartland untouchables.

But if there was one quality most comforting about Farah—teacher, scholar, writer, and leader of Veterans for Peace—it was his intellectual curiosity.

He studied the issue, he tested it, he owned armloads of books on it, he bounced it off allies and adversaries alike, and when he took a case public, it was steel.

"You could disagree with Joe," his friend Jack Miller eulogized, "but you'd better have good reasons—and footnotes."

That the majority tended to disagree with Farah at election time comes as no surprise. Eight decades after the Scopes trial, half the populace still has not accepted evolution. Politicians, eager to pander to myths and taboos, religious and secular, are exalted. It will always be a minority who vote not by faith and reflex but from full conscious involvement, who believe, as Miller said of Farah, "Democracy is not a spectator sport."

When Joe met his wife, Jeanne, in 1982, while both were working for Butler in Robertson Hall, she noticed he had prints of two famous paintings on his office wall—Pablo Picasso's *Guernica* and Peter Blume's *The Rock*. Could it have been a coincidence, she asked the assembled mourners, that she had miniatures of those same works on her desk at the time?

The two masterpieces bracketed the sunlit room where the tributes were voiced. No one could have appreciated more than Farah the conspicuous cover-up of *Guernica* at the United Nations, where it hangs in a place of honor but was not allowed to intrude upon Colin Powell's infamous Iraq war speech. But it was Blume's harrowing portrait of destruction and rebuilding that Joe most cherished, his wife said: "He believed you have to take apart what's not working and put it back together in a better, more meaningful way."

That's no job for whiners or loafers. Joe was the right man for it. He made those around him quit worrying about being wrong. We were blessed beyond price to have him.

Paying for Passage

JULY 13, 2005

Four years ago, she was living in the mountain city of Guanajuato in central Mexico, writing letters to three sons who had gone to Indianapolis for work. Now, Carolina Sanchez is here, a laborer turned striker, taking shifts at a protest encampment on Monument Circle across the street from the largest health care insurance company in the United States.

She hopes the people at WellPoint Inc. will prevail upon the contractor that cleans its offices to improve the lives of its employees. They say it's not their business, but she has come too far for fine distinctions.

She wears a tan Dale Earnhardt Jr. hat and a purple t-shirt proclaiming "Justice for Janitors," with an image of a fist seizing a broom. That's one of her tools, and at age fifty-five, she uses them till she's very tired.

"I wish," the small, stoic lady said in Spanish, "that GSF would treat the workers with respect and pay us what we deserve."

Local labor leaders and clergy have been saying the same, with increasing volume. The Service Employees International Union has been trying to organize the predominantly Hispanic janitorial force here for nearly a year, focusing on the French-owned GSF, the largest cleaning contractor for Indianapolis office buildings. In recent weeks, men and women of the cloth have pressed the issue, calling people such as Sanchez victims of sinful exploitation. On June 29, they held a prayer service at Christ Church Cathedral and then marched with janitors and their children a half block to WellPoint, where they met with executives, the company passing out bottles of juice to the kids.

Officially, it's a stalemate. GSF says it is paying what the market necessitates. It denies SEIU's charges that it is intimidating prounion workers. WellPoint, like Duke Realty and Emmis Communications Corporation, its fellow targets of moral suasion as janitorial customers, insists this is strictly GSF's fight.

With four buildings struck as of Tuesday, and replacement workers cleaning them, a fast is under way. Participants are congregating at a tent the union has set up on the steps of the Soldiers and Sailors Monument. That's where Sanchez was on a gray, humid Monday evening, instead of mopping and vacuuming in Duke's One North Capitol building for $6.50 an hour and no health insurance.

Her son, Miguel, had none with his factory job either. When he was dying of cancer at age nineteen in 2001, she journeyed here.

A tear trailed down her left cheek as she recounted the year with Miguel, his hospitalization and death, the bills she still owes. Her voice hardened as she talked of the three years since, during which she has cleaned at One North Capitol. It's a grind, she said, a seven-hour shift with twelve hours' work. She lost feeling in her right hand from pushing a balky vacuum cleaner and still owes $1,700 for emergency room treatment. Cleaning fluids, she figures, must be why doctors there told her she had the lungs of a smoker.

Right now, she does not know much about her health; she does not go to the doctor. Her money and that of her husband, Felix (he's sixty and lays insulation), goes into a household of six people here and to four grandchildren back in Mexico.

A little more money, a little more time to finish her work, some of the benefits WellPoint is famous for, even maybe retirement. However the organizers and lawyers cast it, she tried the system and now she's on the U.S. pavement seeking a way up.

Is she hopeful?

"Si," Sanchez said with a smile. "Mucho. Mucho."

To a Fallen Comrade
JANUARY 1, 2003

Dear Lynn,

We're off on our first calendar year without you around to turn on the lights in the office, and for sure, it's not looking all that bright out there.

The world is pretty much a mess. Famine, AIDS, and injustice will get worse before they get better. War seems certain, at least in Iraq, maybe India-Pakistan, maybe the Koreas, maybe the Chinas. It's a settled fact of life in the Holy Land. Nobody much believes all this jawing about peace and reason, any more than we believe we really can whup half the world and keep the livin' easy over here.

It's still mighty easy for most of us. You can fight your way to the malls to find that out. But it's not the party it was a few years back. There are more layoffs, more bankruptcies, and of course less help for those folks who never got invited to the party in the first place. The public's in no mood to put more tax money in that ghetto your boy Elvis and your boy Marvin sang to us about. The vibes between the haves and the have-nots are absolutely nothin' sweet right now.

So tell me something new, you must be saying. Friction between poor and nonpoor, black and white, young and wish-they-were-young, made a steady beat in those Lynn Ford columns; and your refrain about senseless killing kept coming and coming as if it might actually sink in some day.

Well, I just wanted you to know somebody's still on the case, as we used to say. The troubles you hollered about are still with us in one form or another, and so are people like you who will sound off about them and wear the labels that result.

I know it hurt you to be called a racist for writing about racism and a loony liberal for writing about love. I got slapped with terms like "bigot" and "hate filled" perhaps more this past year than any other in my too-long career, and here I had thought bigotry and hatred were exactly what I was on the warpath against.

Some of it's just the price of playing the polemics game. Hooray for our side. But some of it is valid, too. You reminded me of that—of the need to examine your own heart, as well as your skill in communicating, before patting yourself on the back about rattling those cracker cages. Having once been the token cracker on a black newspaper, I should not need help empathizing with white folks; but you gave me some, and I appreciate it.

Listening is a commodity in short supply in this land of plenty. So are humor and style, both of which I have missed most keenly this past year, a year scarred by your untimely death in February, by your haunted final months as a victim of the violent crime you cried out against in the newspaper.

You were not a beaten man, Bro. The flair and fury, the Jesse Jackson impressions, the verbal jazz, the unashamed, unfashionable testimony kept coming to the end. I wish we had some of that now as we face a year that surely will shake the soul. The roar of mass discontent and mass destruction will make these little columns on which we expend so much work and play seem like hymns in a hurricane.

On that cheery note, I'll close this correspondence and wish you the very best your faith promised you. If you can put in a word for our planet, please go for it. I'd love to start another year off wrong.

Later.

2

Uncommon Language

Our writers do not tend to hang around here all that much, and they are more honored by the nation at large and its lettered elite than by their hometowns. Nevertheless, Indiana's literary legacy deserves and needs shouting about. Lest that sound like English class homework to my fellow casual readers, be assured that nothing in my decades in this business offered more fun than discovering these half-hidden gems of excellence, eccentricity, and passion, from the Greenwich Village duchess Marguerite Young to the blind Palestinian refugee poet Reja-e Busailah to the motley sharers in open readings at bars and coffeehouses.

The achievement of the poets and novelists is to preserve and exalt the fleeting and ordinary, which explains my appreciation as a practitioner of daily record keeping who aspires to leave a whiff of art on his wares. Seen clearly and handled with care, Etheridge Knight's ancient convict who "sees through stone" can attain immortality; and so can a state hospital patient who is taking a poetry class to save his life.

Ruth Stone's Winter Carnival

MARCH 3, 2000

She laughs. Squeals. Helplessly. Explosively. Discussing her acclaimed poetry, Ruth Stone seems taken over by that bubbly mix of pride and embarrassment a parent might feel at hearing her children praised in public.

But it is not acclaim that delights her; it is poetry. To listen to her is to hear the schoolgirl of seventy-odd years ago who contributed verse to the *Indianapolis Star* and the *New York Times* and lost herself in the inspired futility of stuffing the world into personal pouches of words.

"It's an honor, but it's not a competition," the poet pointedly said of her nomination for the National Book Critics Circle Award. "I don't compete. I just write."

She writes so much, in fact, that she must force herself to make time for the business of submitting her work to periodicals and collecting it into books. Her eleventh book, *Ordinary Words*, published in 1999 by Paris Press of Ashfield, Massachusetts, would win the prestigious National Book Critics Circle Award; and the eighty-four-year-old author has enough material for three or four new ones, she figures.

"I don't think about publication," she said in a phone interview from her office at State University of New York, Binghamton, where she teaches two writing classes. "It's painful to sit down and decide, 'Well, I'd better get some things out.' When you're in a university position, they kind of expect you to publish, you know."

Even in the thinly populated world of serious poetry, many more parties than her university bosses are eager to see Stone publish. A tough, tender, and playful observer of the cosmic game and its dear doomed players, she commands an ever-freshening following with her nonexclusionary feminism and her knack for taking plain language and passing a wand over it.

"Ruth Stone's work is alternately witty, bawdy, touching and profound. But never pompous," reviewer Anita Manning wrote in *USA*

Today. "Her honesty and originality give her writing a sense of youth and newness because she looks at the world so clearly, without all the detritus of social convention the rest of us pick up along the way."

> . . . I take my cup of coffee to a small
> inoffensive table along the wall.
> At the counter the male chorus line
> is lined up tight.
> I look at their almost identical butts,
> their buddy hunched shoulders,
> the curve of their ancient spines.
> They are methodically browsing
> in their own territory.
> This data goes into that vast
> Confused library, the female mind.
> (From "Male Gorillas")

The mind of this latecomer to politicized womanhood has been shaped, and continues to be shaped, by nearly a century of eyewitnessed evolution.

Stone remembers rushing outside to watch whenever a daredevil named Goody Weaver flew his aeroplane over Indianapolis. She remembers listening to a crystal radio, and going to the *Star* to watch her father, Roger Perkins, set metal type. She remembers a strong and lovely mother, also named Ruth, who stayed home with the children.

"I grew up a regular girl, a regular woman. I accepted the male world. I accepted it that men were smarter than I was," Stone said. "The world made that pretty clear."

Born in Roanoke, Virginia, in 1915, Stone moved here with her family when she was three. She attended Shortridge High School until her senior year, when she transferred to Tech to be with friends.

Indianapolis "still holds my heart," she said, and even her latest poetry evokes the city. It was also here, of course, that other worlds began to fill hers, through the books she read omnivorously.

"You want to be moved, don't you? And illuminated. You want to fall into a book that's so real you forget where you are," she said. "I remember reading *Of Human Bondage*. For two days, I didn't move."

While a student at the University of Illinois, Ruth Perkins met a fellow English scholar, Walter Stone. They married when she was twenty and they had three daughters—Marcia, now a guidance counselor; Phoebe, an artist and children's book author; and Abigail, a novelist.

In 1959 in England on a sabbatical from his Vassar College professorship, Walter Stone hanged himself. Forced "to start my life all over at age forty-one or forty-two," his widow went from housewife to working mom, taking teaching jobs at colleges and universities throughout the country, while continuing the writing she had been doing since childhood. Harcourt Brace started publishing her poetry in the 1960s, giving her the cachet to change jobs at will; but financially, it was a struggle.

SUNY Binghamton, where she's been since 1988, is by far her longest stint. She loves the four-day weekend her job leaves her for her own work, she loves the little summerhouse in Vermont, and she loves teaching.

"It takes a lot of energy, but I've got a lot of energy. I really feel the arts are a blessing. It's a great pleasure to me to encourage people to see what creative things they can accomplish when they're not doing the mundane things the world expects of them," Stone said.

Analysis of her own creativity eludes the poet, who's been validated, as if she needed it, with the Shelley Memorial Award, Delmore Schwartz Award, and many other honors.

"It's a mystery," she said." I jump from one way of writing to another. I become someone else all the time. Your understanding— which is never finished—keeps pulling back veils."

In her poetry, the parting of veils reveals, with startling clarity and heartbreaking poignancy, an ever-changing past: a deceased sister who "suffered so; her cells / bursting and burning, eaten alive;" the "rock and rollers on the beach / (who) crash into my, then, middle-aged shocked skull;" the girl in the Marott Hotel lobby in 1930 with all those shoes;

and the husband whose face and odor and Fruit of the Loom shorts keep returning.

> I wore a large brim hat
> like the women in the ads.
> How thin I was: such skin.
> Yes. It was Indianapolis;
> a taste of sin . . .
> Oh mortal love, your bones
> were beautiful. I traced them
> with my fingers . . .
> (From "1941")

It is not as if the past and its vines of sorrow have any tighter grip on the poet than the present. The heron rookeries, bus stations, inequities, and iniquities of the here and now are quarry for her ordinary words, and she defies any fear that the words or the singer might die.

"People come up to me and say this is their first poetry reading— they're not always kids, either—and they never knew poetry readings could be so wonderful, and so funny," Stone said.

Whatever happens in the way of twilight recognition, Stone plans to keep on laughing. She counts herself one of the lucky ones: "It would have been a beautiful world if women had always been educated and had been able to write what they felt. Think of all the genius that never got expressed."

Postscript
JULY 18, 2007

Ruth Stone figures it is about time, and half apologizes in the very next breath for saying so. She need not bite her tongue; and do not worry, she will not.

Being named poet laureate of Vermont, a distinction shared with the likes of Grace Paley and Robert Frost, is a fair climb for an

Indianapolis printer's daughter who mailed verse to newspapers as a schoolgirl.

But that was early in another century and so much has come so late.

Stone has been writing poems for roughly eighty years and publishing them for roughly forty. She has long commanded respect from her peers and the esteem of a community of readers, but she waited until 2000 for a succession of four major-league honors to start kicking in: National Book Award, Book Critics Circle Award, Wallace Stevens Award, and now this, via a phone call June 30 from Vermont governor Jim Douglas himself.

She is ninety-two and has lived in Vermont for fifty years. She has lost most of her vision to macular degeneration and keeps on writing. She knows Paley and knew Frost and is ready to take on their job.

"Don't you think I belong there?" she burst forth in a phone conversation from her apartment in Middlebury. "I've been neglected. Now I'm old enough to speak out. I just haven't been loud and pushy."

Not like that vain, funny guy Frost, for example, who knew how to parlay art into success. "It takes that kind of self-belief," Stone said, a bit wistfully.

But hardly regretfully, because much of the acclaimed work that fills her twelve books draws its poignancy and wit from the female response to male self-promotion and supremacy. In life and art, she has, as they say in country circles, outlasted the jaspers.

Widowed in her early forties, the Tech High School graduate reared three accomplished daughters with a succession of university teaching jobs, writing all the while. Having lived the nation's evolution upward from an unabashed man's world, she could tweak the other half with gems such as this one, titled "Words":

Wallace Stevens says,
"A poet looks at the world
as a man looks at a woman."
I can never know what a man sees
when he looks at a woman.
That is a sealed universe.

On the outside of the bubble
Everything is stretched to infinity.
Along the blacktop, trees are bearded as old men,
like rows of nodding gray-bearded mandarins.
Their secondhand beards were spun by female gypsy moths.
All mandarins are trapped in their images.
A poet looks at the world
as a woman looks at a man.

Pretty spunky for a lady who would go on to win an award named for Stevens and pretty perspicacious too, as the late namesake no doubt would grant. Stone still sees the world with uncanny keenness, notwithstanding the blindness that inspired her most recent book, *Into the Dark.* Next spring will see another book, titled *What Love Comes To.* Next week she will travel to Montpelier with family to accept her title from the governor. She will read one poem. Choosing that from her enormous trove will be an arduous labor of love.

Ruth Stone died on November 19, 2011, at the age of ninety-six.

Norbert Krapf: Words for the Lost
SEPTEMBER 21, 2001

He was about to leave for work from his home on Long Island, twenty miles or so from the World Trade Center, when he heard the news.

From his daughter. Calling from Indianapolis.

Norbert Krapf, professor, poet, and devotee of the sweet life of intellect and family, turned on his television set and watched, over and over, an airliner penetrating a skyscraper just around his corner of the world.

For thousands of people, including scores of Krapf's own neighbors who had employment or business in the towers, life ended. In a sense, life stopped also for him, and the rest of us who survive.

That morning, said the Indiana-born author, "We were in a process of beginning to accept a reality much more horrible than we were prepared to accept. I saw it in the faces on the road."

Krapf went to work at the C. W. Post campus of Long Island University, then drove home after classes were canceled at midday. He took a roundabout route back because the main thoroughfare was restricted to evacuation of the injured. His wife, Katherine, an eighth-grade teacher, and their son Daniel, a high schooler, were safe. But their little community was not.

In the ensuing days, the Krapfs attended a memorial service at the firehouse down the street for a local fireman and policeman who had died in the rescue effort. Then they went to the funeral of a family friend lost in the rubble. He was twenty-nine and engaged to be married.

"It is very difficult. People are having to work through this," said Krapf. "I don't think there are going to be any miracles."

But there will be prayer and poetry. I mentioned to Krapf a book by the religious thinker Walter Brueggemann about the need for a bold, imaginative spiritual language to take over after political wordplay, techspeak, and sermons have failed. The book takes its title, *Finally Comes the Poet*, from a line by Walt Whitman, Krapf's favorite poet and the uncrowned laureate of the American spirit.

Krapf, in turn, recalled his most cherished Whitman line, from "Song of Myself":

"[W]hoever walks a furlong without sympathy walks to his funeral / drest in his shroud."

Whitman, of course, put his body where his voice was, volunteering as a nurse, amanuensis, and untiring friend to Civil War wounded. To many young men, his presence was their miracle.

And who's to say what is a miracle?

Elizabeth Krapf, calling from Butler University, where she is a senior majoring in music, was frantic that morning of September 11. She knew that a good friend, a premed student at Columbia University, was due at the World Trade Center for a meeting at 9 a.m.

It turned out the friend was late leaving home and never got to the scene of destruction. But she went later that day to a hospital and volunteered with the stream of injured. She toiled sixteen hours and returned later the next day.

"She has seen things," Norbert Krapf said, "that she can't even talk about."

The Jasper native, a graduate of Saint Joseph College and the University of Notre Dame, author of *Somewhere in Southern Indiana* and other books, asked me how the horror was affecting people back here. I told him we seemed neck deep in shallowness—flags at ballgames, newspaper columnists prattling about shopping and baking bread as a rebuff to those nasty terrorists. Harking to the image of a young middle-class college student ministering to the wounded in a war zone, I saw my region as a dimension yet more unreal than Krapf's New York, and infinitely removed from parts of the world already ravaged by war and fated for retribution.

Krapf had no answers. He had a poem, still unfinished, that he wrote on the occasion of a funeral, from which I'll rob fragments.

"To hug a mother / who has lost a son," it says, "is to feel how fragile / is the lifeline that / holds us all together."

It is "to hear a sob right / in your ear that comes / from a country worlds / beyond where you stand."

It is "to feel her summon / a strength from beyond"—and to "find the sense of purpose / to walk back to our life."

Yusef Komunyakaa: Country of the Mind

APRIL 18, 1994

Bloomington, IN—There's the random secondhand furniture, including an overstuffed couch in a hue of green not known in nature.

There's the obligatory poster, advertising a reading by the late Indianapolis poet Etheridge Knight.

There's the whole claustrophobic concrete-block space, made closer by walls of paperback books.

The office of Yusef Komunyakaa, associate professor of English at Indiana University, is collegiately correct down to its last low-cost detail, with a couple of exceptions.

His guest is not a student appealing a C grade in a composition, but a newspaper reporter seeking his life story. And when the phone rings, it's the *New York Times*.

"The last few days I haven't been able to write," he says of the fuss about his Pulitzer Prize for poetry, awarded last week. "I'm waiting for the weekend to arrive so I can do what I love doing."

Change, in other words, will not reach to the heart of things.

The Pulitzer, with its $3,000 stipend, and the recent Kingsley Tufts Poetry Award, worth $50,000, will not make Komunyakaa a household name; nor will they likely transport him to a studio overlooking the Pacific Ocean or even nearby Lake Monroe.

Honored poets, like obscure poets, do not get rich. In that sense, and in ways far more profound, one can say the former James Willie Brown Jr., at age forty-six, has not come a long way from Bogalusa, Louisiana.

Like the hard labor of his elders, like the racial terror that underlay daily life, like the blues and gospel music over the radio from Memphis, Tennessee, and New Orleans, Louisiana, book learning shaped the poet and made him value things other than material wealth.

He changed his name as a young man "for cultural and religious reasons," but he could not sever his connection to Bogalusa's working people and its then-segregated schools.

"My teachers had a respect for the intellect, a respect for possibilities through education. It had next to nothing to do with economics," he said. "They believed people should be educated just for respect, just for human potential. My great-grandfather, who was a carpenter and a farmer, kept books. They were smudged with thumbprints from use."

The poet speaks deliberately, in mellow, clipped tones flavored as heavily by Australia as Louisiana. His gray-flecked hair is of medium length. His muted plaid shirt and black wing-tip shoes confound any stereotype of the militant black poet, and so does his work. Its racial identity runs deep and resonates rather than shouts.

"You're home in New York," he writes to an acquaintance from the civil rights movement in the poem "How I See Things."

> I'm back here in Bogalusa
> with one foot in pinewoods.
> The mockingbird's blue note
> sounds to me like please,
> please. A beaten song
> threaded through the skull
> by crosshairs.
> Black hands still turn blood red
> working the strawberry fields.

While he acknowledges race "cannot be denied and is part of someone's psychological shape," Komunyakaa resists having it become a limitation. Sensual as well as cerebral, his work draws from blues singers and the Harlem Renaissance writers, but it also reflects British and Australian poets.

Elsie Otis, eighty-five, remembers her grandson's voracious reading. "He's always been smart," says the Bogalusa resident, who watched him on television the other night. "And I'm glad for him."

Komunyakaa has been many places since Bogalusa, including Australia, the homeland of his wife, fiction writer Mandy Sayer. Most notably, he has been to Vietnam, where he won the Bronze Star and barely escaped with his skin.

"Thanks for the tree / between me and the sniper's bullet," he wrote in "Thanks." "I don't know what made the grass / sway seconds before the Viet Cong / raised his soundless rifle."

It was not until after Vietnam, 1973, that Komunyakaa enrolled in college, not until several years after that that he gained the confidence to publish poetry, and not until 1987 that he was able to make Vietnam a subject. Then, he says, "all these images just started pouring forth."

His Pulitzer Prize–winning book, *Neon Vernacular*, contains poems from his 1988 volume *Dien Cai Dau*, one of several powerful literary works turned out in recent years by veterans of a war officially long over.

"I think we're still trying to sort through the pathos, trying to make some sense out of that moment in history, how it informed our lives," Komunyakaa said. "We're trying to give some shape, some human shape, to that war, trying to understand ourselves and how it changed us."

An award for a Vietnam-related poem called "Facing It" helped bring Komunyakaa to the attention of IU and, in 1987, to its employ.

"I've thought for a long, long time Yusef was one of the best poets writing right now," says fellow faculty member and poet Roger Mitchell. "When the award comes in our own backyard, it's a boost for the writing program, the school, the state. We're extraordinarily lucky to have him."

During breaks from classes, interviews, readings, and seminars, Komunyakaa is working on three collections of poems and guarding his privacy. He will not say much about his current personal life, and if he enjoys being asked over and over how it feels to be a winner, he hides it well.

"Often, you're here in this kind of ethereal, abstract place. Sometimes it doesn't seem to have a floor," he said with a laugh. "So the prize tells me basically that 'Yes, you have been able to give your life over to something that is important, and maybe it's important to others as well.'"

Brian O'Neill: Write Your Name

SEPTEMBER 17, 1995

Madison, IN—The poets adjourn to the open porch of A Ward, the addictions unit, where their cigarettes sharpen a damp morning breeze off the Ohio River.

They sit in a tight knot, on chairs and swings and the concrete floor, folding and smoothing their sheets of lined notebook paper, surrounding Brian O'Neill.

"Tim, you're one of our veterans, one of our published poets," O'Neill said. "Why don't you read first?"

So Tim Frye, a young man with a benign, unshaven face and lush curly hair, reads what he's written over the past twenty minutes. It is called "Every Morning":

> I awaken from my warm night
> of sleep, hear the big furnace
> blowing hot into the room.
> While the room fills with warmth and
> the window frost begins to melt
> in the new sun
> I can smell the coffee and
> bacon and know that my grandmother
> has been up for hours working to push
> the day into motion . . .

"Nicely done," the man in the middle exclaimed. "That was a fine piece of writing. Great details. Let's give him a round of applause."

It is called positive reinforcement. As poet in residence at Madison State Hospital, O'Neill throws it around like Tootsie Rolls from a parade float. If he were merely patronizing the mental patients and substance abusers who populate his workshops, he would not brag about their work to the rest of the world as he does.

"Have faith in your language; have faith in your voice," he told them. And he rewards that faith not just with praise but with publication, in a series of inexpensive booklets and newsletters from which he will recite to strangers as proudly as if this were his own prize-winning verse.

"In here you get down to basics quickly," he reflected in a conversation between classes on the vast, baronial old campus. "I think that makes for better writing."

For Frye, the basics are drug addiction and manic depression. At age thirty-five, he might be taking his last shot at building an independent life.

"When I got here in April, I didn't want to be part of no poetry class," he said. "But I tried it, and I got into it. It's a release—good memories as well as bad memories. It helps you to understand what makes you a person."

Therapy is not all Frye wants out of poetry, nor is it all O'Neill seeks. They want better and better poems.

"Some stuff comes naturally to me," Frye said. "It just pops into my head. Brian helps me structure it. He helps me go a step beyond."

A graduate of the University of Notre Dame with a master's degree in creative writing from Indiana University, O'Neill provides writing programs for schools, libraries, and the Madison hospital through a cottage business called Let's Write About It Inc.

The scarcity of jobs in academia drove him to venture out on his own, where the clientele are generally below college level and, in some cases, functionally illiterate. Yet he has never lowered the quality of his reading list nor his zest for wrestling with words.

Compact, lightly padded, thinning on top, O'Neill at forty-five has the quick gestures and garrulous punch of a second baseman at spring training. He wears round wire-rimmed glasses, tan Dockers, and tennis shoes on his Friday morning rounds, part of a weekly overnight routine that started with a commute from his home in Bloomington for Thursday evening workshops.

His last stop is North Two, the building for female schizophrenics, where he lets himself in with a key, saunters into the dayroom, and snaps off the television.

"You've been cookin' lately," he said to the dozen or so women seated around the bright, roomy lounge as he passed out paper and pencils. "Valerie! Look me in the eye. Look me in the eye. Look me in the eye. Are you gonna tell me you can't write today?

"Valerie, I'm going to make you a bet. Eventually, you'll write a poem for me, before we're both dead."

Valerie does write a poem. So do eight or ten others, despite all the moaning about not being in the mood, not knowing what to write about, not knowing how to write.

"You know how to spell your name," O'Neill gently insisted to a young woman with folded arms. "Write your name down."

Before any poetry is done, O'Neill is prevailed upon to play the piano. After rendering "As Time Goes By" and "Summertime," and "You'll Never Walk Alone" on the unevenly tuned upright, he starts his group off with the same Robert Hayden poem he used as a model in the addictions unit.

"It's a beautiful poem. It's a thank-you poem," he said. "It's a poem to his father thanking him for something he had taken for granted. We all have someone in our lives we want to thank. Now's your chance to write it down. Maybe it's someone you can't thank anymore."

The room falls silent and pencils scratch, just like on that providential first night in 1984, when O'Neill took his consulting business to Madison State and was escorted to a ward for violent men.

He read Philip Levine's blue-collar poem "On the Street Corner" to them. He found out most of them had spent nights on street corners, and yes, they had something to say about it.

This morning, Terry Pollard wants to say something about her grandfather.

"It doesn't rhyme," she confessed.

"It doesn't have to rhyme," O'Neill replied.

She reads:

"I thank my grandfather for those winter days when he would tell me when I was a little girl to look out the window to look at the winter snow that would always make me happy. I would play and play. I thank you."

"That was excellent," the teacher said. "That was the best thing you've ever written for me. I told you if you kept writing you'd get better, and what happened?"

She smiles tentatively. She is twenty-four, dark-eyed and slender, dressed like a college student in a flannel shirt and black high-top sneakers. Like many here, she has not seen her family in a long time.

"I wasn't good at writing," she said. "He said to keep going and I'd be good. I got better. . . . My mom was a professional at it. She wrote about me being a queen and my brother being a king. She passed away. I wish I could find that poem."

To O'Neill, who has had scores of his own poems published in literary journals, poetry cannot be too personal. Sick or well, a writer uses poetry to "make sense of the past and imagine a future," he said.

"The idea is to get people to write in images—the texture of experience. Literature is lived experience, not a chronology of facts," O'Neill said. "And it provides a catharsis, even for somebody like Sandy, who never writes about anything but the food she eats."

O'Neill has received awards from Governor Evan Bayh and the Indiana Humanities Council for his eleven years of teaching at Madison State, the only Indiana state hospital with a poet in residence. Perhaps his biggest fan is Jerry Thaden, superintendent of the hospital, who has fended off attacks by budget cutters on O'Neill's $20,000-a-year program.

"The writing is a metaphor for work," Thaden said. "Prior to the 1970s, when the antipeonage movement came along, state hospitals were communal. Patients did farming and so forth. That came to be seen as involuntary servitude, and we were unable to use work as part of communal life. Writing is a substitute for that. For whatever reason, it's not valued by the world the way lawn mowing is, so you don't have to pay for it. It fills a void. It gives them a product of being here."

Thaden agreed with O'Neill that the writing is therapeutic to the extent it's not labeled as therapy.

"The best way to change our lives is to examine them and write about them in a humanistic rather than a medical setting," O'Neill said. "I see their writing not as evidence of pathology—you know, are they progressing or regressing—but as their work."

In the addictions unit, he lets Leo Hill know the work is valued. Solemn-faced, quiet, and wearing a ponytail and a vivid tie-dyed

T-shirt, Hill sits on the cold porch floor and reads from his poem called "Freedom:"

> . . . We threw our heads back
> And great torrents of laughter
> Exploded
> Yes, that day we were free . . .
> . . . As the evening closed you were
> home as was I
> The next day I awoke to a
> new freedom
> and you passed away to yours
> If only I had known
> I would have said Good-bye

"Damn, you can write, Leo! Zow! I'm a professional writer, and when I get sweaty hands, that's a bad sign somebody's writing better than me. Tone it down, Leo," said O'Neill. Leo permits himself a grin. He says he has kept a journal for thirty years, since he was ten. He and his journal have another month in Madison State, and maybe then he'll start the future he is trying to imagine.

"It's easier for me to get my emotions and feelings out by writing than it is by talking to people," he said. "If nobody listens, my journal always does."

Gale Christianson: The Devil's Work
JULY 18, 1999

Terre Haute, IN—Gale E. Christianson is a slight fellow with fine gray-brown hair who wears delicate-framed glasses and once spent five years wrestling with a giant.

"Newton damn near killed me," he told a visitor to Indiana State University, where he teaches history and writes internationally acclaimed books. "When I was finished, I told my wife, 'If I can write that one, I can write anything.'"

He laughed. For an author seven times over, he has a huge capacity for self-effacement, something not found among Sir Isaac Newton's ample gifts. When this "plodding scholar," as Christianson describes himself, undertook to tell the life of the immortal genius and to explain Newton's monumental *Principia Mathematica* to lay readers, "I would have sold my soul to the devil to get through that."

Well, he made it through without Faustian cost, as far as he knows; and *In the Presence of the Creator: Isaac Newton and His Times* entered the world in 1984 to generally favorable reviews. It was his second book and established the loquacious and industrious professor as a master of the art of making science history interesting to the educated general reader.

His new book, *Greenhouse: The 200-Year History of Global Warming*, carries an ecstatic blurb from public television science expert David Suzuki and was positively reviewed in the *New York Times* by the renowned urbanologist and author Witold Rybczynski.

A solid wall of evidence for human complicity in global warming, *Greenhouse* bears the same trademark Christianson stamped on his Newton biography, his study of astronomer Edwin Hubble, his life of natural science writer Loren Eiseley, and all his other books—it is alive with personalities, places, and gee-whiz details.

Take, for example, one Jean-Baptiste-Joseph Fourier, who conceived the model of the Earth as a bell jar that holds in the sun's heat. He narrowly escaped the guillotine during the French Revolution and spent his last years wearing a wooden box lest he topple over and suffocate from chronic rheumatism.

The kind of sweet melancholy that drew Christianson to Eiseley's poetic essays surfaces again with Fourier, starting *Greenhouse* on a note that says this is not another think-tank lecture on the editorial page. "My goal," Christianson said, "is to keep the reader turning the pages. . . . It's not a work of genius, but it's a challenge."

There he goes again. Christianson, who teaches a full course load and could get away with less if he wished, thinks of himself as teacher as much as writer. He almost never applies the term "author" to himself.

His modesty and his big ideas have the same roots. Born fifty-seven years ago in Iowa farm country, he experienced what he calls an isolated childhood. He was barely conscious of television before his teens, rarely traveled, and never visited a museum before his twenties. But there were books, and spoken stories, and parents, grandparents, teachers, and peers who brought words to life. Like virtually all his classmates, Christianson went off to college.

He came to ISU in 1971 fresh out of Carnegie-Mellon Institute, where he earned a PhD in history. He needed to publish and had no interest in the dry, narrow esoterica of the academy. Looking for something wider and flashier, he tried the universe. *This Wild Abyss: The Story of the Men Who Made Modern Astronomy* demonstrated his attraction to genius and his flair for catchy titles.

Convinced that "the biographer needs to be hidden off stage," Christianson played hooky in one of his books, a collection of personal essays about the perils and pleasures of his trade. Its title, *Writing Lives Is the Devil!*, is a quotation from the great novelist Virginia Woolf, who was driven to despair by her only attempt at biography.

Free to use the first-person singular ("the most disgusting of pronouns," in his quote of Edward Gibbon), Christianson shares fascinating anecdotes about combing archives, approaching subjects' widows, sweating out reviews, and so forth. He tells of his vow, when he lost his grandfather at age seven, to capture lives dear to him. Since then, owing to the years he's spent with their ghosts, the famous have become like family to him. And like family, they have not been romanticized—nor even necessarily liked.

The brilliant Hubble was a racial bigot who affected British mannerisms down to the wearing of knickers. The lyrical Eiseley was crabbed enough to declare that the students shot down at Kent State University had it coming. Newton, the biographer's object of greatest satisfaction, played politics for keeps. "Newton was a son of a bitch in many ways," Christianson reflected, "but he had that redemptive quality of genius."

Newton's biographer is content to be able to bring the fire to the rest of us. Acute readers may see a spark of genius in the ability to transform an icon into a story, but Christianson will have none of that.

"I've been lucky. I've gotten some good reviews," he allowed. "I've learned a tremendous amount as a writer."

If a biographer a hundred years from now wishes to expand upon that un-Newtonian epitaph, the Terre Haute professor can just bedevil him from beyond the grave. He has seen that done.

Verse Jones

SEPTEMBER 11, 1999

"We free singers be, baby."
Etheridge Knight (1931–91)

Mostly, they move by night, unseen and unheard by the world that knows them as the truck mechanic or the bank worker or the elementary schoolteacher or the high school student.

They roar like Kay Cheek, taking on life-and-death issues in a smoke-choked side room of Lockerbie Coffeehouse at Michigan Street and College Avenue.

They purr like James Officer Jr., celebrating black womanhood amid the white tablecloths and dark drums of the Omega Conference Center at Thirty-first Street and Sutherland Avenue.

They snarl, like Joshua Strodtman stalking Nancy Reagan, hiss like Suzanne Evans exposing unsavory sex, growl like J. R. Depp attacking racism, strut their splendor like Nicole Rose all but caressing the microphone:

I wanna be in a room I just love
I wanna change the air
I wanna make you thirsteeee like salt water
I wanna be where I'm not.

They are on the prowl for applause, for laughs, for shock, for reinforcement, for camaraderie, for converts, for romance, and for the ancient thrill of the spoken word, these participants in Indianapolis's open poetry reading scene.

They are far more varied than they are numerous and far more likely to be unpublished than published.

But hey, unpublished is not so shabby. That's how Homer and the Psalmists got their start.

"There is a need on the part of all human beings to tell our stories and . . . to have personal involvement in the telling," said Officer, president of Midtown Writers Association. "To truly read the story, we have to see the individual who tells the story."

The burly forty-nine-year-old mechanic/poet/percussionist, whose organization principally serves black writers and performers, notes that the oral literary tradition is especially vital to people of African descent.

"Open mike goes right along the lines of how we have evolved. But humans as a whole need to bring their energy to the words," Officer said. "They need to have the personal satisfaction of knowing the story was told correctly."

With donated space and volunteer help from the Omega service organization, Midtown has held open readings at the conference center, under the name Kafe Kuumba, for more than two years.

With Cheek in charge, readings have been held for about the same length of time at Lockerbie, also in donated space. "Our problem was that there was no continuing, ongoing reading you could count on," the twenty-two-year-old bank employee and Indiana University–Purdue University at Indianapolis student explained. "We feel a sense of urgency now to make sure people support all the readings. You're not a traitor because you go to that reading instead of this one."

Both gatherings, currently the only local weekly open readings with any age on them, take place on Thursday nights. Each drew upward of forty people on a recent evening, though attendance varies widely.

Both are heirs to the Beat movement of the 1960s and to a thin, dotted line of Indianapolis bar balladry going back to the early 1970s—the Hummingbird, the Alley Cat, the Slippery Noodle.

A veteran of those venues, John Clark, publisher of the poetry magazine *pLopLop*, started a monthly open-mike series, Open Borders, at Borders Book Shop in Castleton, in 1992. Deborah Sellers now directs the sessions, held the third Friday of every month.

Another monthly series, Cafe Li'ture, meets on fourth Sundays at X-Pression Bookstore on North College Avenue near the hip hub of Broad Ripple.

Unlike some other cities, Indianapolis has not yet embraced the slam, that boisterous and sometimes ugly sport of dueling poets.

Officer is polling to gauge interest in starting a slam at Kafe Kuumba, but there is no doubt any such competition would follow Marquess of Queensberry rules. Under the black-green-and-red pan-Africanist flag at the Omega, no poet need fear humiliation.

"It's very welcoming," said Nicole Rose, a twenty-four-year-old grade school art teacher and sculptor who rendered three expressive love poems at Kuumba on a recent night. "It doesn't matter if you're fantastic or you're horrible. They make you come back."

That doesn't mean there is no friction and spontaneous commentary, but the familiarity among most participants tends to convert potential tension into general liveliness.

Much of the interruption at Lockerbie is punctuation—"Yeah!" and "Whoo!" and "You're a bad m----- f-----, T. J.!"

At Kafe Kuumba, there is also lots of back and forth, some of it very much part of the communal artists' plan. One of the readers Officer has to cut off on a recent night is Ben Khayil, who conducts a question-and-answer session with his audience on religion and the history of oppressed people.

"Brother! Five minutes!" Officer told the young zealot in the blue and gold African robe. "You do that every week, man."

For many poets, the problem is not stopping, but starting. While a Joshua Strodtman can saunter up to the stage carrying a guitar and launch into "Nancy Reagan, you ruined my generation" as blithely as if he were in his kitchen, others read haltingly from sheets and journals held close and tight. Some are barely audible. Some confess to nervousness. Some say "That's it" when they have finished.

"It's great to see people come out all intimidated and a year later sound like established poets," Deborah Sellers said.

Her own experience at Borders is a case in point: "Before, God forbid anyone would call me to go first, or to go after someone really good. Now, it's 'Who cares. Let's do it.'"

"Let's do it" also applies to the material, of course. No grades are issued for polish and structure, and much of the fare is raw expression—erotic longing, lovers' quarrels, rants about the sorry state of the world, indulgence in language that Mom is not out there in the smoke at 11 p.m. to hear.

There even are surprises for the truly jaded. Rhyming poems. Recitations from memory. Cleo House, who bills himself as the Dark Knight, bursting into an a cappella hymn, "Jesus is the center of my joy."

In the spirit of the late, renowned Indianapolis poet Etheridge Knight, who founded the Midtown Writers Association and considered "just plain people talkin' " to be the purest form of poetry, organizers of readings say the freedom they foster is necessary to get the art form off dusty library shelves and into real life.

"Poetry started out as an oral tradition and people forget that," Sellers said. "And the [published] poetry shows it."

The personal poetry of open mike also calls into question what real life is, in Officer's view.

"We are more than the sum total of our education, our bank accounts, and our jobs," he declared against the insistent backdrop of drumming and amplified speech. "Who knows what happens when they leave here? They go back to their jobs, but then what? They live to come to Kafe Kuumba. It's like a religious experience."

Etheridge in Rough Draft

SEPTEMBER 29, 1999

He was a poet highly praised and a man deeply loved.

He also was a drunk, an addict, a thief, a jailbird, a liar, a swindler, a first-degree womanizer, and a betrayer of the finest friends anyone could ask for.

We know these things about Etheridge Knight not just from gossip, of which there's plenty, but because he told us.

The award-winning, much-anthologized, much-traveled troubador of black pain and persistence never let himself off the hook in his nakedly personal art.

Some of his titles were confessions—"Feeling Fucked Up," "Junky's Song"—and so were many of his lines:

> . . . she opened
> to me like a flower
> but I fell on her
> like a stone . . .

Nearly a decade after his death from cancer at age fifty-nine, the open book that is Knight is being read and discussed in his familial hometown of Indianapolis and far beyond.

Butler University's Irwin Library has his posthumous papers, adding itself to the primary archive at the University of Toledo. The material ranges from the literary to the mundane to the shockingly intimate.

His sister, Eunice Knight-Bowens, has her ninth annual Etheridge Knight Festival of the Arts scheduled for next spring.

Two literary journals, *Callaloo* at the University of Virginia and *The Worcester Review* in Massachusetts, have devoted recent issues to Knight and have published posthumous poems.

A book of interviews with him, *Breathing from the Belly: Freedom and Poetry*, edited by former Indianapolis poet Jean Anaporte-Easton, is in the hands of the University of Michigan Press.

Boston-area poet Elizabeth McKim, Knight's last companion, has a manuscript in the works about him that includes interviews and original poems.

What it all means, said Fran Quinn, Butler's poet in residence and Knight's former literary executor, is a shot at immortality—a chance that a black ex-convict who took poetry to the bars and barbershops will stand alongside James Whitcomb Riley and Kurt Vonnegut Jr. as an Indianapolis literary institution.

"We need some distance from his death," Quinn cautioned. "But he will be re-evaluated, and his name will sing prominently."

Some of America's biggest poetic names—Gwendolyn Brooks, Robert Bly, Galway Kinnell—agree. Their admiration for Knight's earthy, rhythmic verse evolved into friendship, a common building block in literary reputations. But the work, Knight's friends assert, has its own merit.

"It will endure, the very best of it," said Donald Hall, one of the nation's preeminent poets and anthologists. "Mostly the poems from prison—'The Idea of Ancestry,' 'Hard Rock.' I read 'As You Leave Me' to my classes a lot."

Knight, Hall said, was a bridge to African American life, and to poetry's oral beginnings, for a white Harvard-educated poet who lives in New Hampshire and had to have "funky" defined for him.

"He had his difficulties, as you and I know," Hall added. "But he was generous in many ways."

"Difficulties" does not begin to describe the Knight laid bare in the recollections of those who knew him and in the more than ten thousand pages of material in the Butler archives. Ranging from handwritten drafts of poems to requests for welfare assistance to notices from creditors to correspondence with publishers and universities, the collection is most remarkable for personal letters whose intensity and sexual explicitness mock the hushed, antique-furnished top-floor sanctuary where they are housed.

Sometimes in outsized script, sometimes in single-spaced typing that goes on for a half-dozen pages per epistle, wives and lovers pledge their devotion to the poet and vent their anguish over his wandering, philandering, drinking, and drug abuse.

"I'm glad you're in there. At least for the period of time that you're hospitalized, no alcohol is killing those brain cells," a former wife wrote Knight.

Later, exasperated with his infidelity, she declared: "I can never be one watering hole among many, as you have so aptly coined the phrase."

Another lover, in successive letters, says "Have a good day and kiss me every / where," "Where are you Etheridge Knight?" and "I hated that you stole from me."

She means her money, not her heart.

"You had to protect yourself from Etheridge," Quinn said. "I frisked him when he left my apartment. I wouldn't talk to him for a while because of the way he treated these women who were my friends. But he and I were friends at the end."

The women in Knight's life were many. Four stand out. He married San Francisco poet Sonia Sanchez in 1969, shortly after leaving Indiana State Prison, where he served six years for armed robbery and found the poetry that "brought me back to life."

Freedom meant access to drugs, which cost Knight his marriage and, some say, his chance to build a large body of work.

He divorced Sanchez in 1970 and four years later married Mary McAnally, a political activist and poet in Tulsa, Oklahoma. She reared their adopted children, Etheridge Bambata and Mary Tandiwe McAnally Knight, the latter of whom inspired Knight's renowned poem "Circling the Daughter."

That union died in the latter 1970s, during which time Knight lived with Charlene Blackburn of Massachusetts, mother of Isaac BuShie Blackburn Knight, his only biological child.

His companion during most of the 1980s was Elizabeth Gordon McKim. Though they had separated by then, she joined him in Indianapolis after he returned here in 1989 for hospitalization after a car accident in Philadelphia. The cancer was diagnosed here, and McKim, along with Sanchez and Belzora Knight, Etheridge's mother, was at his bedside when he died on March 10, 1991, in a subsidized apartment for elderly and disabled persons on Massachusetts Avenue.

In his last year, Knight made "completions," McKim recalled. "He went back to places he had left in disarray. He saw people who loved him. He said good-bye. There was something so loving about Etheridge then, such tenderness."

Heroin, she says, was the tragic flip side to a people's artist who was loved for his openness as much as his voice. "There was always that desperation," said McKim. "There was the impulse toward generosity and poetry and his calling; then there was the impulse to get the next fix. It was amazing that he maintained."

Weeks before Knight's death, Hall, Bly, Brooks and other notable writers came here for a fund-raising tribute that woke up the city in general, and Knight's family in particular, to the prominence of this winner of the American Book Award and author of five books of poetry.

To be sure, Indianapolis was not the place of his roots. Born in Corinth, Mississippi, he was in the army when his family moved here in 1949. He divided the remaining four decades among Indianapolis, Memphis, Philadelphia, San Francisco, Boston, and various other places, including prisons and rehabilitation hospitals.

"He was a wandering man," Hall said. "It doesn't surprise me the Indianapolis community didn't know him till he was dead or almost dead. I'm not indignant about that."

Knight-Bowens, whose primary literary experience was writing gospel-related plays, lost little time attacking the name-recognition issue. She started the annual festival in 1992, and while it has not been embraced by the literary fraternity, she insists Knight was not something out of his family's league.

"His mother [who died in 1997] was a poet," she said. "He was raised in a family of artists. This is nothing unusual. Etheridge just happened to be the only one out in the arts community."

In the meantime, Quinn and Etheridge's sister, Janice Knight Mooney, as literary coexecutors, carried out the poet's wish to have his papers sold and the proceeds disbursed to his three children and seventeen nieces and nephews.

Quinn wanted very much to keep a hometown writer's artifacts home, something Indiana has failed to do with its literary greats. He also sought to improve Butler's historically weak rapport with the black community.

The Ward M. Canaday Center at the University of Toledo already was the site of a Knight collection and had the right of first refusal for the material he had upon his death. Quinn says Toledo was uninterested because it had been scammed by Knight with some bogus papers, but Toledo archivist Barbara Floyd said the university simply found too little literary material in the postmortem batch to justify paying for it.

The Irwin Library's director, Lewis Miller, said the $14,000 acquisition, completed in 1997, is part of a mission to "refocus the Special Collections area to make it accessible and useable for students and to make it more identified with the local community."

Knight-Bowens said she is "OK with Butler" as a repository of her brother's papers, but would have preferred an even more accessible place, such as Central Library.

As for the graphically unflattering nature of some of the private keepsakes that now are on public view, she declared the family's pride in the poet will prevail.

"People die and things start coming out of the closet," said Knight-Bowens. "We didn't have to deal with that. Everybody knew Etheridge was a drug addict. Everybody knew he would steal to support his addiction. Everybody knew he'd been in jail. Everybody knew he loved women. Nothing bad could come back and hit us after his death. He protected us."

Will history preserve him?

Quinn says he and Bly joked after the funeral about moving dirt from Riley's grave to Knight's little by little until Knight's usurped Riley's as the highest spot in Crown Hill Cemetery.

In an interview with the *Indianapolis Star* weeks before his death, Knight said he cared only about what happened while he lived. Among his Butler papers, in the corner of a letter from the Houghton Mifflin Publishing Company, is a notation in black ink:

"If I'm dead when you Read this, don't pay much attention to me. Pay Attention to live Poets, Poets preferably of your generation / time."

Marguerite Young: Swan Song to a Radical
OCTOBER 23, 1999

She was the red-tressed toast of Greenwich Village, a pal of Gloria Vanderbilt, a teacher of Kurt Vonnegut Jr., the author of a 1,200-page novel that's drawn higher praise from higher places than perhaps any other book rooted in Indiana.

When she was brought home to Indianapolis to finish her final masterpiece and her life, she was Aunt Margie, who wanted her writing pad, her books, her dolls, and a hug from her niece against the coming night.

"She was unbelievable," Daphne Nowling said of Marguerite Young, who died November 17, 1995, in the room Nowling painted red for her. "She was a genius, definitely. I just wish I was a writer and had the words to describe her."

There's no shortage of writers to describe Marguerite Young. Vonnegut called her "unquestionably a genius." The poet Mark Van Doren said her "eloquence has no parallel among the novelists of our time." Critics compared her 1965 novel *Miss Macintosh, My Darling* to the work of James Joyce, William Faulkner, and Herman Melville.

Alas, the huge, roundabout *Miss Macintosh* was, like Joyce's greatest novels, more praised than read, and the chain-smoking, shawl-draped New York Bohemian figure who wrote it was as little-known in Indianapolis as was her book's phenomenal narrator, Vera Cartwheel.

Her effusive obituary in the *New York Times* was the length of a book compared to notices in the hometown press. Thirteen people attended the local funeral of the woman who, in the words of a national critic, "added epic grandeur to the philosophical novel."

Perhaps her craggy profile will rise now.

Four years after her death at age eighty-seven, thirty-five years after *Miss Macintosh*, and more than a quarter century after she began work on a biography of Eugene V. Debs, her book about the Indiana labor giant is in print.

The recent release of *Harp Song for a Radical*, by Alfred A. Knopf Publishing Company, crowns a massive effort by Young's old friend and fellow writer Charles Ruas to reduce a 2,500-page manuscript by more than 75 percent.

"Terrible, terrible," Ruas said of the task of deciding what to leave out. "I wanted very much to keep the breadth and perspective of Marguerite's genius," he added in a telephone conversation from New York. "Her mind could take in everything—Utopian settlements, Debs, the railroads, the union movement, the Socialist Party. . . . This is a forgotten chapter of American history."

Daphne Nowling, who delivered the immense manuscript to Ruas after her aunt died, agreed with him that publishing realities precluded using more than a fraction of Young's precious words. Nowling has sold thousands of pages of drafts, notes, and poems, much of it done with Young's trademark red marking pen, to Yale University, the repository of the writer's papers. More posthumous work may be forthcoming.

Ruas is exultant about the work at hand. He said Young's elegiac saga could restore Debs to his lost place as a champion of the common person and "change people's understanding of their country." He lavishes words such as "legendary" and "wonderful" upon the author, a lifelong teacher of writing who "gave of herself without restraint."

He also made the point that Young, a product of Shortridge High School and Indiana and Butler Universities, "always considered herself a Hoosier" even though she left here as a young woman and hobnobbed with the cosmopolitan likes of Gore Vidal and Anais Nin.

"And she felt that to be a Hoosier was to be a poet," Ruas said.

Nowling, who went to New York in 1993 to bring home the ailing aunt who had shown her high society when she was a teenager, is happy Young's work and name will endure.

Her regret, having taken Aunt Margie into the lives of her and her three children, does not involve anything of epic grandeur. She's only sorry Aunt Margie was not in the red room when death came.

Though the invalid artist was not able to see much of her native city, her niece will remember her return as a happy time. She carries the image of Aunt Margie on the bed, knee raised, staring into space, and then scrawling with her red pen, the instrument that lifted her to the level of Faulkner and Joyce.

"She was always writing, and in that poetic style," said Nowling. "She spoke that way a lot, too—'Darling this' and 'Darling that.' She was so funny. She was cute, too." In her aunt's last months, "I got into bed with her a few times and snuggled her up. She would say, 'Darling, I'm going to die.' I would say, 'What do you want me to do, Aunt Margie?' She would say, 'Hold me in your arms.'"

Lilly Library's Paper Wealth
JANUARY 7, 2000

Bloomington, IN—She calls herself one of the Fatheads. Her group gets together from time to time, by phone or over lunch, and talks about other people's business—often, quite personal business.

Inevitably, the conversation comes around to money, as in, "So how much did you turn the Allen Ginsberg papers down for?"

As director of a world-class repository of rare books, historic documents, and important writers' effects, Lisa Browar of the Indiana University Lilly Library finds herself in a rivalry with the Yales and Harvards of the world.

It is a friendly rivalry, involving as it does people who pursue matters of the mind—and flaunt a funny moniker for their obsession.

"We're not collecting trophies," Browar said. "We're here to put together a rich research resource for scholars. That said, there is competition. But even if you lose, you know it's gone to a good home, so to speak."

With more than 400,000 books, 7 million manuscripts, and 150,000 pieces of sheet music, not to mention artwork and furniture and other keepsakes, the Lilly Library is the safe, eternal home of armloads of Western culture's offspring. Manuscripts, letters, and other leavings from Upton Sinclair, Kurt Vonnegut Jr., Nadine Gordimer, Athol Fugard, Sylvia Plath, Galway Kinnell, Dylan Thomas, Patrick O'Brian, Virginia Woolf, and hundreds of other prominent writers fill the hard-lidded cardboard boxes in its climate-controlled stacks.

First editions of hundreds of books, whose authors range in age and grace from John Bunyan and Geoffrey Chaucer to John Le Carre and Ian Fleming, rest clean and dry along narrow aisles.

Two of film director John Ford's Oscars are here. So are more than 8,000 children's books collected by the late Muncie heiress Elisabeth Ball. And one of the world's largest collections of miniature books, scores of which would fit in one's palm.

In the Lincoln Room just past the lobby, a bust of the sixteenth president, carved by the Mount Rushmore artist Gutzon Borglum, overlooks a glass-encased Gutenberg New Testament dating from about 1455, the dawn of movable-type printing in Europe.

Alongside the New Testament is one of the twelve pages that were missing when the Lilly acquired the book in 1958. When the so-called Prodigal Leaf turned up in the possession of Christie's auction house in London in 1997, the Lilly won it for £15,000 (roughly $25,000 American) and held a champagne-and-cake party for its homecoming.

"It's not like day trading on the stock exchange," Browar said. "But some days it can be very intense. We have a budget. We must prioritize. Offers to sell the Vonnegut and [contemporary novelist] Tim O'Brien papers came the same month. We had to pass on Tim."

No wonder. Vonnegut's papers cost $225,000, or nearly one-third of the Lilly's annual acquisition budget, which is a mix of university funds and endowments created with donations.

While buying and bidding keep Browar and her curators on the phone and the Internet, life at the Lilly is blessed with many gifts, both of specimens and of money.

Private donations to the IU Foundation financed the 1958 purchase of a large collection from Chicago magnate George Poole that included the Gutenberg New Testament and the first three editions of Chaucer's *Canterbury Tales*. The total tab was $450,000; today, Browar figures, the collection would fetch several million dollars.

The Gutenberg came before there was a Lilly Library, but just in time for the donation that made the place happen.

During the latter half of the 1950s, Josiah K. Lilly (1893–1966) of the pharmaceutical family gave the university his collection of more than 20,000 books, 17,000 manuscripts, 52 oil paintings, and 300 prints. It remains one of IU's most prized gifts.

With the rare book and manuscript section of the general library thus pushed past bursting, then-IU president Herman B Wells, whose thumbprint is on so much of IU's history, urged construction of a separate repository. Lilly Library opened in 1960 and, like the rest of the library system, is now bursting. New storage facilities are soon to be built.

Meanwhile and beyond, Browar and her staff of twenty full-time librarians plus student assistants must contend with sorting, analyzing, cleaning, restoring, and cataloging material that may range from a few fragile sheafs in Writer Y's case to a truckload in Writer Z's. Former U.S. Senator Birch Bayh's papers take up 1,200 boxes. (Yes, they let politicians in—1940 presidential candidate Wendell Willkie and former governor Paul McNutt).

Space being at a premium, the question of what to discard, or what not to accept in the first place, always pertains. Often, Browar said, it's a "crapshoot" whether a given writer will be important in fifty years.

In cases where staying power seems assured, there's still the need to sift through his stuff. Vonnegut's 1940 report card from Shortridge

High School is in his Lilly papers; but what if he had included a 1963 grocery list?

"Different archivists give different answers," said Browar, a 1973 IU graduate who headed the rare book division of the New York Public Library before coming to Lilly in 1998. "You have to appraise the material in its totality. What's there and what's important to the author's life and work? Some things are usually not retained. Before we get it, there's some selecting out while it's in the author's possession. Once it's in the library, any culling ought to be minimal."

Browar makes sure to warn authors (and their widows and widowers) that Lilly has no exit. If there is a drippy, scandalous love letter in the mix, it will drip and shock perpetually for all who wish to witness.

As it was under Browar's immediate predecessor, William Cagle, and his predecessors, Cecil Byrd and David Randall, the Lilly is a working library. University classes ply its holdings and it stages three major exhibitions of artifacts every year. About four thousand people annually, a fourth of the library's total visitors, satisfy their research needs and/or curiosity in the monitored but very public reading room.

Nor can a writer or his heirs control the flow of personal information into the archives. It can come from any direction.

The Lilly, for example, does not have short-story master Raymond Carver's papers, but it does have Gordon Lish's. When a reporter for the *New York Times Magazine* came across marked-up drafts and pleading letters from Carver in those files a while back, he found fuel for the suspicion that Lish, famed as the editor who launched Carver's career, rewrote Carver's early drafts to make those celebrated stories his own. That was distressing to Carver's fans and family, but priceless to students of contemporary literature, including Fatheads.

"I like to say I get paid to go through other people's mail," Browar confided with a laugh. "But the interest isn't prurient; it's archaeological. We're talking about preserving cultural memory."

Felix Stefanile: Hoisting the Hyphen

MAY 6, 2000

West Lafayette, IN—Chances are their parents were not born when Felix Stefanile (pronounced "stefan-EE-lay") published his first poem, and the cavalcade of jeans and backpacks trudging past his walk-up flat in the spring sunshine may be grandparents themselves when he ceases to be read.

Not that the eighty-year-old Purdue University professor emeritus makes a big deal about his own literary longevity. Others do that for him. His many honors include the John Ciardi Award for achievement in Italian-American poetry. His books carry blurbs from X. J. Kennedy and Dana Gioia, stars of the genre.

Stefanile's hope is wider. It extends to the hundreds of poets he and his wife, Selma, have nurtured in their role as publishers. As the typed note above the doorbell proclaims, theirs is the home of *Sparrow*, an annual compendium of formal (rhymed and metered) poetry they started in 1954, making it one of the oldest poetry magazines extant.

A speck in a sky filled with small literary journals, *Sparrow* is in good company, historically speaking. Ralph Waldo Emerson's *Dial* had a hundred paid subscribers when it closed down, but it had Emerson and Henry David Thoreau on its pages.

"John Ciardi speaks of the difference between horizontal and vertical popularity," Stefanile told a visitor to the dark, cozy, book-lined apartment in the heart of campus. "There are some writers who sell to mass audiences and are forgotten in three years. Emerson is read to this day."

For more insight into the mind of Stefanile, consider a writer who was read virtually not at all in her own day. Stefanile's new book of poems, *The Country of Absence* (Bordighera Press), begins with an essay that compares Emily Dickinson with today's rap artists, noting that the "public authority of taste and decorum" would not allow her into print because "she would not write like a lady." Miss Emily made power out of powerlessness, he said, and so have the rappers, and so did the immigrant writers before them.

Stefanile learned about being the butt of power whenever he ventured out of his Long Island neighborhood and submitted himself to White-Anglo-Saxon-Protestant scrutiny as a kid. But he also learned about the power that could be his from a kindly and literature-loving high-school teacher named Mr. Aronowitz, from the books of Henry Wadsworth Longfellow, and from the works of Dante Gabriel Rossetti, who taught young Felix that his people had their own Longfellows.

The budding poet went on to City College of New York, becoming, by his reckoning, the first Stefanile in seven thousand years to attend college. He studied Italian and Latin, the former of which was put to use when he was drafted into the army during World War II and assigned to interpret for Italian prisoners.

A portrait of him painted by one of those prisoners adorns his living room wall. The hair is dark and thick instead of white and recessive, the jaw is smooth rather than seamed, the eyes gaze free of today's thick glasses; but the subject is far from wistful about it. "He made me look like Mussolini," he cracked, the New York accent as pristine as the picture.

The war inspired some of Stefanile's most powerful poems, covering issues of friendship and loss ("The Dance at St. Gabriel's"), racial discrimination ("Hubie"), and romance and xenophobia ("Ballad of the War Bride"). The war is also part of that communal stream of consciousness—Joe DiMaggio, corner pizza parlors, red-brick cathedrals—that is somehow both quintessentially American and indivisibly Italian.

"To say that Felix Stefanile is the most significant living Italian-American poet does not do full justice to his achievement," Gioia once wrote. "When he writes so movingly of living between two languages and two cultures, he not only presents the immigrant's situation but the human dilemma."

Stefanile began publishing in commercial magazines in 1950, supporting himself as an office worker with the New York Department of Labor. He met a coworker named Selma Epstein in 1952, and they were married a year later. They started *Sparrow* a year after that as a sanctuary against what Stefanile called "the free verse orthodoxy" ruling modern poetry. (Let it be noted that he, no reverse bigot, often writes in free verse himself.)

Whence the name? "Sparrows are Catullus, sparrows are William Carlos Williams, sparrows are all over poetry," Stefanile said, but that is not the reason.

"I chose the name because the sparrow is a hardy bird. It doesn't go away. It's not a seasonal bird. It may die in the winter, but it won't go to Florida. We intended to be here to stay. Selma and I made a promise and we've kept it."

In 1961 a Purdue administrator who admired *Sparrow* invited Stefanile to serve as a visiting lecturer for a year. His classes turned out to be popular both horizontally and vertically, so he was asked to stay on. In 1969 he became tenured. "PhD level with a bachelor's degree," he chuckled. He retired in 1987 and has remained employed, busily, if not lucratively, as poet, publisher, translator, and Italian American avatar.

"The Hyphen," as writers refer to the ethnic label, incites much debate and consternation these days, and Stefanile resisted it for many years ("Let's face it: Breaking into the mainstream is not for sissies.") But he's come to find traditional identity liberating rather than limiting. Like small publishing, it is a way of swimming in the mainstream under one's own power instead of just floating along.

"The hyphen," said the poet, "is long pants for the human mind, rather than shorts."

"The Dance at St. Gabriel's"
(for Louis Otto)

We were the smart kids of the neighborhood
where, after high school, no one went to school,
you NYU and I CCNY.
We eyed each other at St. Gabriel's
on Friday nights, and eyed each other's girls.

You were the cute, proverbial good catch
—just think of it, nineteen—and so was I,
but all we had was moonlight on our minds.
This made us cagey; we would meet outside
to figure how to dump our dates, go cruising.
In those hag-ridden and race-conscious times
we wanted to be known as anti-fascists,
and thus get over our Italian names.
When the war came, you volunteered, while I
backed in by not applying for deferment,
for which my loving family called me Fool.
Once, furloughs overlapping, we met up,
the Flight Lieutenant and the PFC;
we joked about the pair we made, and sauntered.
That Father Murray took one look at us,
and said our Air Force wings were the only wings
we'd ever earn. We lofted up our beers.
Ah, Louis, what good times we two have missed.
Your first time up and out the Germans had you,
and for your golden wings they blew you down.

3

Uttered in the Heat

Polemics have been the signature product of my labors over the millennium-crossing years, and the reception has been as polarized as the society itself. I'm an oasis in a reactionary desert. I'm a clueless leftist misfit. I'm just plain mad at life.

Certainly, I've been a full and fierce participant in the political conversation of the Clinton-Bush-Obama-Bayh-O'Bannon-Kernan-Daniels era. I like to think I've taken a global view from my Heartland vantage point and confounded those who identify Hoosier values with complacency, superstition, fear of change, and acquiescence to power. I hope the cries I have raised over the Iraq wars, the death penalty, religious demagoguery, and other epochal issues have cut through the noise of our nightmares and awakened common dreams. I hope my occasional forays into satire have proved therapeutic for someone other than the author. I'm aware, as much of this book will reflect, that I speak against the unceasing background rumble of 9/11.

Day of Nightfall

SEPTEMBER 12, 2001

It is not supposed to happen in the United States of America, this feeling of mass vulnerability, this sickening sensation that we are indeed all in it together and the power structure we have put in place cannot save us.

Day to day, our worries about epidemics and nuclear weapons and the anger and megalomania that seethe within and all around our island of peace and prosperity tend to be abstract, academic, the stuff of cocktail parties and quickly forgotten editorials.

Then, as we amble through another day like the day before, the blow comes.

Two generations ago, it was the patrician tones of a president yanking us toward the ornate radios where we were used to gathering for our comedy nights, excoriating a fellow mighty nation against which we would have to go to war.

A generation later, it was fuzzy black-and-white televisions interrupting quiz shows to inform us a young president had been murdered.

Each time, we felt not just furious and bewildered and frightened, but abandoned. Irrationally, we thought we'd had a bargain that we could sleep because our protectors never did. If enemies could stage a sneak attack on a military base, if they could get to the president himself, where was the safety we had taken for granted?

Tuesday, we arrived at work or glanced across the living room, and found on the nonstop news screens not a distant hurricane or football highlights, but hell hitting home—New York City's proudest buildings in flames and crumbling. The Pentagon likewise struck by a renegade aircraft. Bodies, God knows how many. Amid the visual and informational chaos, report after report of more terrorism, more sweeping protective reactions, airports closed, schools locked down, a body politic gone from quarreling over tax rates to a posture of war.

And war against whom, or what? In a world so small, with bitterness so deep and lethal technology so sophisticated and available, finding and punishing the perpetrators of these incomprehensible atrocities will not compare in complexity to our response to Dallas or even to Pearl Harbor. We will not send our sons off to die in trenches for our security, in all likelihood. But we will know now, as we did not believe then, that security is a luxury that cannot be sustained.

We have been struck before by domestic terrorism of the modern kind, the kind most Americans unfairly identify with Arabs. We prosecuted perpetrators of the 1993 World Trade Center bombing, and we executed Timothy McVeigh, whose crazed act in Oklahoma City was at first widely assumed to be the work of foreigners, of Arabs. We have tightened security at airports, at federal buildings, in civilian workplaces, and schools.

And now this nightmare.

We cry out—for the victims, for vengeance, for a clear victory over whichever individuals and nations did this. And though our cries are just, we know down deep that what we want is a security and a simplicity that cannot be enjoyed anywhere in a world that has never not been at war, on some scale, somewhere.

When we talk with our children about this dastardly and desperate act, we must take care not to perpetuate the delusion that safety is a birthright for some people on the planet. Children who are growing up accustomed to bombs, and children who have no concept of such a life, are all subject to the same viral insanity that made the century just past the bloodiest in human history.

The writer Carol Bly says people who are facing a mass threat, such as pogroms and ethnic cleansing, need to develop a crisis mentality that would shield them from the complacency that leaves them hoping it all will just go away. It is time for our fear and our fury to form themselves into such a mind-set. Just what expression this new awareness would take, I would never presume to say, certainly not now, in the smoke and carnage that assail me from the screen on the wall of this place that yesterday was safe. I would dread seeing the expression reduced to just going off to war. I would only wish it could be that simple.

For now, my only response is the simplest. I will do what my high school biology class did at that moment I will never forget, on November 22, 1963. I will draw close to those I care about, and pray.

New Wars, Old Looks
OCTOBER 12, 2001

The destruction of a distant, destitute, and virtually defenseless country by the world's dominant military power has not amounted to a big deal as yet in the place from which the assault is launched.

Oh, they cheered the news of the bombing at a stock car race (still special, that South). The television networks and newspapers tweaked their stars-and-stripes logos again. Child-development experts recycled their reassurances to American parents (which is fitting, inasmuch as those neighborhoods are not under daily bombing runs). They have even called up the reserves, though it's hard to imagine whom those people would actually fight.

For the most part, though, life has gone on in the USA, except for New York City, which looks much like Kabul but for the more confined area of damage. We are assured by our government that the human toll from the September 11 atrocity has not been nearly matched in the pounding of Afghanistan; but as the president has admonished us, this will be a long one.

The implication is that Americans will be called upon for sacrifice on the order of World War II and Vietnam. But in fact, it has been more than a generation since the United States threw down the gauntlet to a militarily competitive nation, and not even the most reactionary of our leaders since then has seriously broached the idea of a revived draft.

Under Reagan, under Bush I and II and under Clinton, the pattern has held: High-tech punishment of weak adversaries, conducted by professionals, with a low ratio of facts (i.e., casualty figures) to ad hominem propaganda. We had to bomb, you see, lest Gadhafi or

Saddam or the Taliban outdo Hitler, or at least oppress women. Never mind that Saddam, for example, remains in power while a million of his people, by United Nations estimates, have died as a result of war devastation and a continuing embargo. Those still alive should be grateful we took on their despot, as Afghans should give thanks for the food we're dropping with the ordnance.

Let's be clear: If Osama bin Laden and his associates are involved in the despicable acts of September 11 and other lethal terrorism, then the world must set aside its grudges for a comparative minute and cooperate to bring them to justice, however messy that process would surely be.

But to proclaim so, and to give George Bush and his aging architects of failed violence carte blanche to bomb and invade sovereign states for not turning the suspects over, are not the same thing.

We would not bomb Mexico or France if it happened to have a "leftist" regime that demanded unequivocal proof of the quarry's guilt. We would discover diplomacy.

We certainly gave no ultimatum to China when it was holding not an alleged Saudi murderer but several American airmen, taken into custody after their reconnaissance plane was brought down. Our resolute, Churchillian president of current media portrayals apologized to the Chinese and shortly thereafter asked Congress to extend trade relations with them. Guess why.

The reality is, we make war on Afghanistan and Libya and Grenada and Iraq because we can—militarily, financially and, yes, politically. The American public will stand for it, at least until U.S. casualties reach a certain level. The villains will make for Internet jokes and toilet paper imprints. If war were declared (and it's never quite officially declared) against China or Russia, the sound of throats clearing would be deafening.

The oh-so-odious Taliban would have converted American conservatives to feminism if Paula Jones had not already done so. But exactly how its ouster would stop terrorism has not been spelled out. In fact, Americans have been warned to expect more terrorism now because more untrackable folks out there will be angry at the United States.

Yet the crusade rages on. While Americans generally are behind it so far, it also seems to be behind them. Maybe they notice the new war looks an awful lot like the last couple. They cannot help but notice over there in the rubble of Afghanistan, where Mister Rogers is not heard.

Beating Mississippi

MARCH 9, 2005

Forget about budget shortfalls, Medicaid, and school funding. You do not really know Indiana politics until you've experienced an Eric Miller show.

The unchallenged general of God's First Indiana Regiment held a rally to "defend marriage" Tuesday that rattled the stained-glass windows and shook the marble walls of the Statehouse Rotunda, sending hundreds of followers on to seek "victory" over an enemy who ought to be very, very scared, as well as angry.

Gay Hoosiers and their allies, several hundred strong in their own right, massed outside in protest and worked their way inside to try to spoil Miller's party. Some ugly confrontations ensued. But neither their numbers nor their decibels were any match for the multigenerational faithful who packed the main floor, the stairways and both upper levels of what Miller reminded them in his almost unvarying shout was "Your Statehouse."

They shared the building with a host of beaming elected officials and religious lobbyists arrayed across and around the dais, as well as with the insurgent protesters and busy state troopers. But if anyone owned the place over this hour and a half, it was Miller. Even the sign behind him—"Eric Miller and Advance America Invite You to Your Statehouse"—said so.

It might have been his for longer than a piece of an afternoon, had he not lost last year in the Republican primary for governor. He and his backers have warned Governor Mitch Daniels since then that they still wield the evangelical vote and must be reckoned with. Tuesday, Miller basked in the glory that affords, drawing ovation after pounding ovation, as did his fellow speakers, from a crowd that acted as though stopping gay people from getting married amounts to turning the Visigoths away from the gates.

Tall, slender, dark-suited, with an ever-smiling ruddy face, Miller could have passed for a minister presiding at a funeral, until he reached the microphone.

"You're in the right place at the right time for the right reason," he thundered to an answering roar. "It's right to support marriage between one man and one woman."

Senate Joint Resolution 7 would do more than that. Approved overwhelmingly by the Senate and now before the House, it not only would forbid homosexuals from getting married but would deny civil unions and domestic partnerships as well if Miller and his legislative allies have their way.

Why is such vanquishing of a vastly outnumbered enemy imperative? Miller and his peers answered that with a litany of generalities, platitudes, blandishments, and canards, all of them explosive applause lines.

"Your children are at risk."

"We don't want to be like Massachusetts."

"Churches could be sued if they didn't grant membership to homosexuals."

Few catch phrases went unuttered or unappreciated. Attorney General Steve Carter said marriage law means to serve "biological parents" and their "natural-born children." Micah Clark of the Indiana Family Institute trotted out "Sally and Susie" and "Sally and Steve."

But it was Miller, shortly before sending the troops off with a round of "God Bless America," who brought down the house by throwing down the gauntlet. Noting that southern states have had the biggest majorities against gay marriage and that Indiana's constitutional amendment must pass another legislature and a referendum, he proclaimed: "You, the voters, are going to beat Mississippi in 2008."

Seeding Storm Clouds

MARCH 27, 2011

The Indiana Senate will take our state to the brink of civil war this week when it votes, by a biblically thumping margin, to inscribe injustice into the Indiana Constitution.

The Senate Judiciary Committee set the stage last week when it endorsed the ban on same-sex marriage and, for good measure, refused to make an exception for civil unions, under which gay couples enjoy various benefits of family partnership such as inheritance and hospital visitation.

By voting to deny any and all government recognition to potentially thousands of loving households, the people's elected servants put the lie once and for all to their hollow refrain that they seek to defend "traditional marriage" and not to attack anyone.

The Catholic Church, which sanctimoniously blesses this appalling agenda, and the Catholic state attorney general, who piously promises to defend it, ought to at least stop kidding themselves and us, their fellow Catholics, that they are following the Gospels.

It is a Christianity Jesus would not recognize that fuels this crusade, and it is a religious war that will ensue.

After the full Senate approves House Joint Resolution 6, the proposal will rest until the next legislature is elected in 2012. With the GOP in charge of redistricting, the required passage by a second legislature seems a sure bet. Then the matter goes to the final stage, a referendum, where the ugliness will spill over.

Gay and lesbian Hoosiers, with their many friends, will take to the streets, demonstrating that they have children, church memberships, paid-up taxes, and no horns. "Family values" fanatics will hold thunderous rallies against the diabolical menace of full citizenship for their neighbors. They'll demand "tolerance" for their "principles" and denounce the anger they stir in those they pronounce beneath them. Heavily funded propaganda will enrich the news media across the spectrum.

Polite conservatives will continue to wring their hands about this "distraction" from economic issues and point out that same-sex marriage already is forbidden under state law. The Chamber of Commerce, which would stamp a bar code on life itself, will lament the dampening effect of antigay politics on recruitment of educated workers. Church leaders will wring their well-washed hands and call for civil dialogue.

Who will say discrimination is discrimination, and no law, no constitutional amendment, and no process that perpetuates it is acceptable?

Not Governor Mitch Daniels, a better friend to gay and lesbian citizens than any Democratic governor, but a presidential aspirant with enough battles on his hands.

Not the Democratic Party, sadly. While the Republicans bear the guilt for elevating bigotry to top priority, the party of the people has hardly fought for gay people with the same ferocity it has exhibited—admirably—for teachers and other unionized workers.

Remember, the Democrats postponed their filibuster flight long enough for the House to pass some proposals, including the marriage resolution. The self-anointed champion of the downtrodden, Representative Pat Bauer, voted for it.

The dogs of war, thus, appear loosed. Polite society is unmoved and shaken. It shall be a time of moral testing, much like that which prompted William Butler Yeats to write a lasting epitaph: "The best lack all conviction, while the worst are full of passionate intensity."

Who Will Stop This Hard Rain?
MARCH 13, 2011

It looks as if the governor and I both misread the climate.

I wondered at first why he was asking his troops to hold off on right-to-work legislation, inasmuch as they were riding a right-wing Republican wave into the 2011 Indiana General Assembly session.

Turns out the union-busting push, subject of dire warnings by

Democrats before the election, was the spark that drove the party of the people out of the Statehouse and the state.

If Governor Mitch Daniels hoped that lowering that single red flag would lure the minority back to take its thumping, he was in for a surprise.

Most of us were, even the House Democrats.

Protest actions, to be sure. Demands for concessions, absolutely, from one of the most antagonistic agendas the party of big business and sectarianism ever has unfurled.

But holing up in a motel in Illinois for weeks into the session, with no end in sight? That speaks to a force greater than the people involved. The conventional scoldings about childish losers and their obligation to get back to work do not fit this phenomenon.

You do not need a weatherman to tell which way the wind blows; and this one is a gale even stolid Hoosier politicians could not withstand. In Indiana, in Wisconsin, in Ohio, and across the map, they've been radicalized by heavily financed Republican hubris.

Not coincidentally, so have thousands of respectable working people, who find themselves braving rain and scorn to join a fight that's spilled over from the ballot box. Again, they did not start it.

With collective bargaining, public institutions, and secularism on the run, the Mitch Danielses and Scott Walkers and Chris Christies and their industrialist backers are poised, if not for the kill, then for the permanent crippling of these Democratic and democratic mainstays.

Their tactic, pardon my Greek, is to demonize the *demos*. Find school failure where it does not exist and blame unionized teachers. Lower the investment in the schools, divert their tax dollars to private, even for-profit schools, and call it philanthropy. Label prison guards, firefighters, and welfare caseworkers overpaid aliens when they earn no more than their neighbors, and often less, for comparable work.

Make those neighbors jealous of working people who make a decent living, rather than angry at CEOs who walk away with millions from a wrecked economy.

It's a war, waged with lies, fraught with high stakes, not given to Geneva Convention protocol. Still, I cannot say I am far enough to the left to be comfortable with the Comfort Suites caucus.

The Democrats lost the election. They're going to lose some more after the Republicans redraw the district boundaries. They appear to have a choice between facing bitter reality and forfeiting their legitimacy. They're not revolutionaries, this isn't Egypt, this too shall pass.

But how long? Long enough for a lot of suffering, for which many Democrats insist they would be culpable if they were to give in now—and I grant their sincerity even as I doubt there's more they can accomplish shouting into the wind.

"How long? Not long!" the Reverend Martin Luther King Jr. declared, on his way to winning a war for hearts and minds. Indiana and the nation need such a conversion on the part of those with the upper hand. Is there a lightning strike in this stormy weather?

The Word Becomes Flash

JANUARY 16, 2011

Yea, though I walk through the valley of the shadow of reality, I shall fear no evil, for television news hath me covered.

If there be a suspicious fire in any garage along even the least traveled of alleys, they shall be on the scene.

If Colts fans are holding forth in either celebration or mourning in the loudest of bars, my journalistic champions shall make their shouted inquiries heard.

If an assistant to a county surveyor dares use the office credit card to refuel his or her personal vehicle, the mighty microphone shall bring down its wrath.

And let no weather—not intermittent rain, not a dusting of snow, not potentially skin-reddening unseasonable warmth—seek to invade the viewing area without detection. For lo! It shall be tracked.

They are tracking the precipitation for me.

They are on top of the fires and shootings for me.

They are following the high school "sexting" story night and day, as they have been for weeks and weeks, ever since they were first to break the story, and they will tell me how to protect my children from what they, exclusively, have learned.

They will fight for me and for my family against the schemes of the most diabolical siding salesmen and not-really-homeless panhandlers.

Keeping my family and me safe is their duty, and woe be unto the inner-city carjacker, Great Plains frontal system or Black Friday mob of bargain hunters that would presume to evade their vigilance.

And what does escape their twenty-four-hour-a-day scrutiny?

Boring stuff, pretty much. Taxes, education, art, power, and how it is purchased. Propaganda and how the powerful transmit it through the "objective" news media. Corruption above the level of petty embezzlement. That's heavy fare, hard on your tummy. Gives you a headache. When it comes to enemies of these dimensions, my high-gloss and high-volume heroes in local television news leave me pretty much on my own.

"It sounded like information, basically," the essayist George Saunders wrote in his acclaimed book *The Braindead Megaphone* about a sample broadcast. "He signed off crisply, nobody back at NewsCenter8 or wherever laughed at him. And across our fair city, people sat there and took it, and I believe that, generally, they weren't laughing at him either. They, like us in our house, were used to it, and consented to the idea that some Information had just occurred. Although what we had been told, we already knew, although it had been told in banal language, revved up with that strange TV-news emphasis ('cold WEATHer leads SOME motorISTS to drive less, CARrie!'), we took it, and, I would say, it did something to us: Made us dumber and more accepting of slop."

O, he of little faith. Does he not contemplate a life without shopping tips, without knowledge of drive-by shootings and their leg wounds, without commentary on the Colts from his fellow citizens?

Does he take for granted those who stand on the wall and spare him that trek through endless desert?

Surely, they shall keep the heretics in their prayers, knowing full well the reward for their work.

It All Seemed So Real
DECEMBER 1, 2000

When Al awakened, he found the smiling faces of those he loved arrayed around the bed.

Bill. Tipper. Joe. Professor Marvel, who'd helped Al invent the Internet.

Toto's muffled yelps could be heard from inside the Social Security lockbox Al kept on his nightstand.

"You've been out since the big twister hit way back on November 7," Bill explained to him.

"For a while there," Tipper added in a quavering voice, "we thought you were going to leave us."

"Oh, but I did leave you!" Al cried. "I went far away, to a very strange place. It was wonderful, with Disney World and the most delightful football, but I was awfully frightened and I just kept saying, 'I want to go home. I want to go back to Washington.'"

Chuckles erupted. But it all still seemed so real to Al—how he had been hurrying home to beat the storm in the flying machine he invented when he crash-landed in this magical land where the grass was cut short as a carpet.

He remembered clear as day how the people approached him, driving little carts and wearing visors. Though they hauled bags of clubs, they were joyously friendly. The stoutest and rosiest of them came forth and read a proclamation.

"As mayor of the Democrat City, in the county of the land of Oz, I welcome you most regally . . . "

Another rotund fellow interrupted.

"But we've got to verify it legally! To see. If the GOP. Is positively.

Absolutely. Indisputably. Indivisibly. Undeniably . . . DEAD!"

Only then, said the denizens of the Democrat City, could Al fulfill his wish to go home to Washington.

"And how do I do this?"

"Oh, you don't have the power," the mayor said. "Only the Supreme Oz can declare the GOP dead, and you must travel to the Tallahassee City to beseech his help. But watch out for the Wicked Secretary as you follow the Yellow Pad Road. She has seized our ballots that broke the spell of the GOP. She must want them very badly."

Al set out. He walked for days through grim forests, beset by the horrible cackles of the Wicked Secretary overhead, avoiding distractions such as the three wayfarers who sought radical medical procedures but were not seniors.

When at long last he entered the Tallahassee City, Al was addressed in a voice like a thunderclap.

"I am Supreme Oz, the great and powerful. Who are you!?"

"I am Al, the tall and alpha. I seek your help in returning to Washington, where I might fight for Tallahassee City."

"Very well. I will grant your request. Provided you bring back the ballots of the Wicked Secretary and have them all counted for me."

"But, but . . . that might take weeks. And I'd have to destroy her, or at least obtain injunctive relief."

"Go!"

And indeed Al stormed the all-but-impenetrable castle of the Wicked Secretary at the head of a phalanx of attorneys. He returned in triumph to Tallahassee City, where the counting commenced.

Snip, snip here,

Poke, poke there,

A couple of dimpled chads;

That's how we pass the weeks away,

When Al's facing uphill odds . . .

Then it came to Al, safe in his bed, what had been so frightening about his adventure. It was not the Wicked Secretary, determined to keep the GOP alive at any cost. It was all those ballots, thousands of them, falling like snow over a poppy field, demanding to be counted and counted again until every Munchkin in Oz was recognized as a fully enfranchised American. Only then could Al, heroic, depart.

"And now, here I am. Don't you believe me?" he pleaded.

"Al," Bill said gently. "The only Tallahassee we know of is in Florida, and your opponent conceded the moment the networks called it for you."

"You mean?"

"That's right, Al. You've been the president-elect since about the time of the cyclone."

"Jeepers! Then I'm glad, because this is home, and you're all here, and I'm never going away again!"

"Can we count on that?" Tipper joshed, to the merriment of all.

Getting Tough with Granny
NOVEMBER 24, 2000

Killers have come and gone since Lula McNeil entered the state penal system in 1989.

The mother of ten and grandmother of eight will be seventy-two when her release comes up in 2003.

"They're calling me the dope-dealing granny," she sighed, "that they've got to lock up and throw away the key."

Her offense is dealing in cocaine, allegedly less than one ounce, total, on three occasions in September of 1987, in and around her home in the 3100 block of North New Jersey Street.

Her claim is that she made only one transaction and that authorities tried to portray her as a "kingpin" even though she had no prior record for dope trafficking. "But any amount," she conceded, "would be wrong."

Her mistake, in hindsight, was pleading innocent. Her codefendant got a much shorter sentence by throwing himself on the court's mercy. The judge would not grant McNeil a delay when she called from a hospital on the opening day of her trial to say she was sick.

She made it for the second day of the two-day bench trial in Marion Superior Court, after which she got four thirty-year sentences to be served concurrently. Half that thirty years must be served before parole ordinarily is possible. With credit for 191 days in jail awaiting trial, McNeil figures to serve fourteen years, more than many a homicide convict. That's the drug law the public is deemed to desire.

She has glaucoma, bronchial trouble, and other ailments. She has completed a long list of service and rehabilitation programs at Rockville Training Center. She has pleaded that children need her at home. But her petitions for clemency and sentence modification have been denied.

McNeil has no lawyer. She's had bad results from four of them, including one who committed suicide after being disbarred and another who is in prison for killing his wife.

McNeil was not lucky. She was not privileged. She was not smart. And she was not innocent.

Does she deserve to spend more than a decade of her golden years behind bars, knitting teddy bears for state troopers to give to traumatized children?

Marion County Deputy Prosecutor Brian Jennings, who put her there, thinks so. Working people in inner-city neighborhoods want pushers gone, and that's his job as head of the Metro Drug Task Force.

"Dealing drugs at 30th and New Jersey in front of her grandchildren," he said. "Nice lady."

The lady also is a statistic. Women are the fastest-growing segment of the Indiana prison population, increasing nearly 600 percent over twenty years to more than 1,300. Older inmates also are more numerous than before. The principal reason, the Department of Correction says, is more drug prosecutions and longer drug sentences.

So now we have overcrowding. We have the need for new facilities such as Rockville, more than an hour's drive from the city where many inmates' families live. We have inmates with the kind of family ties young male convicts don't have. McNeil has missed the funerals of two daughters, two sons, a son-in-law, a brother, and a grandson during her stay. Before then, she was the de facto parent of some of her grandchildren.

"She was the backbone of our family," said a daughter, Rhonda Ingram. "She held us together."

Across a visitors' table in a gleaming mall-like complex planted in western Indiana farmland, the grandmother talks nonstop of the wrong she believes she suffered from the justice system, and of her efforts, mostly by letter and phone, to keep her grandchildren out of the system. She asserts she would be out by now if lawyers and clerks had not mishandled her court papers and if various officials had not ignored her pleas of hardship. But she's through applying for shortened time. No use, she says.

"One time when I first got locked up it made me bitter. I had to adjust to the fact I'm here," she said.

Is it especially hard not seeing her grandchildren on days like Thanksgiving?

"I don't celebrate holidays," she said. "I celebrate every day I have."

All the Rage
JANUARY 21, 2001

In a society bent on drugging, counseling, and preaching its way to earthly bliss, someone needs to put in a kind word on behalf of wrath.

From time to time, I'll receive a complaint that some commentary in the paper is flawed, not just by illogic or by dishonesty, but by anger.

Never mind what the words say; somebody at the keyboard or easel has a problem, the reader discerns, and needs a timeout.

I even had a caller say the other day she avoids articles that show anger lest she herself become angry, in violation of her religious beliefs.

I have to tell you, this criticism kind of ticks me off.

What it implies is that the work of an editorial writer is not all that important, because there are no evils abroad in the world that are worth getting all that upset about. Tell that to the man who saw red when he saw the money changers in the temple.

Strange bedfellows, old-time salvation theology, and new-age therapy. In all seriousness, I do not wish to disparage this particular reader's concern, nor her faith. But I see in this renunciation of the honest emotion of anger a modern fixation on personal "happiness" at the sacrifice of social duty.

Newspapers and television are evidence enough. Compare the amount of muckraking and hard-core commentary with the space and air devoted to movie stars, weight loss, child-rearing advice, and shopping.

You can turn on Jerry Springer and laugh at people who are mad as hell, but you are hard pressed to find anything designed to make you mad. Mad like Jesus was, that is. Righteously angry. Incensed by more than the high price of your gas bill.

When the news media took on the great social issue of Bob Knight, we discussed his anger and quoted experts on anger management. I even heard that effete coinage "anger management" in Tate's Barber Shop on West Tenth Street, of all sensible places. Coach himself, refreshingly enough, pretty much said he just got bleeped off at bleeping bleepers who did not know bleep. Anger was both blessing and bane to his controversial career, but it was a distant second to ego as the source of his downfall, and ego is something we have enshrined.

I trace the current demonization of anger to our old pal Phil Donahue, granddaddy of the therapeutic talk show. Even in his own 1970s heyday, he was parodied for trivializing people's genuine political differences with some variant of "I sense anger here." In the era of his heiress, Oprah, you probably get worked over by security if you dare leave the show with any anger on your person.

There have been times when anger has been widely considered a civic virtue. It shook transplanted Englishmen out of their complacency in the 1770s. It drove us to take on the Axis powers, and to pass civil rights laws. It has sparked more than one renaissance in the arts. It gave us Mothers against Drunk Driving and "Letter from Birmingham Jail."

Now, we are paying the equivalent of a wartime budget to an army of secular and religious gurus who would help us get rid of our anger. Their work is valuable as far as it goes. It goes too far when it bids us quit trying to change the world. We were placed on this Earth to try, and most likely fail, to change it.

The late Congressman Mickey Leland probably would be alive today if he had not gotten so steamed about starving children in Africa that he flew humanitarian missions there in dilapidated airplanes. His death made others mad, so the push up this mountain of a problem continues.

I read once that you can measure a person by the size of that which makes him angry. Starvation in a wealthy world makes me angry. Nominees for cabinet posts who laud the Confederacy make me angry. Good liberals who blind themselves to the plight of the Palestinians make me angry. I think those objects of ire are a big deal, and I only wish I had more rage to vent upon them.

Whew, I feel better. Not for too long, I hope.

Wake for a Collective Soul
MARCH 16, 2001

In the depths of a night on which the state will exact a death for a death, life persists along the gold coast of North Meridian Street.

The strollers and joggers with their pedigreed pets have long since abandoned the sidewalk as midnight takes us into Wednesday, leaving a knot of shivering souls at the corner of Forty-sixth Street, some wearing dark winter coats and some in red T-shirts imprinted with "Stop Executions Now."

Here and there a car rockets past, inches away off the low curb, punctuating the presence of death that keeps bringing these people back to the lawn of the Governor's Mansion. Here and there a car passes with a honk of support. A stretch limousine even pulls to a stop, revelers rolling down one of the smoked windows to discuss capital punishment with a couple of demonstrators.

Mostly, the great main drag of Indiana is dead, its black, damp expanse reflecting red and green stoplights like buoys on an empty lake. The only signs of life at the house where Governor Frank O'Bannon lives are dull lights in downstairs windows and an unmarked State Police car parked crosswise in the driveway, pitch dark inside but occupied.

"He's the problem," Charlie Kafoure said, jerking his thumb over his shoulder toward the silent mansion. "If he kills Gerald Bivins tonight, which he will, then that study commission means nothing."

These veteran opponents of capital punishment—Kafoure, JoAnne Lingle, Joe Zelenka, the Reverend Bill Munshower from Saint Thomas Aquinas Catholic Church around the corner, and a dozen others here tonight—have stood vigil in worse weather, including December nights. Usually they've had more company.

This time, the man awaiting killing half a state away in Michigan City is a "volunteer," a nonappellant, which both inspires less protest and excuses the refusal to grant a stay.

Yet a diverse, expert advisory panel is supposed to be studying the fairness of Indiana's application of the death penalty that O'Bannon helped write into law. The people on the curb do not understand how even advocates of capital punishment can justify carrying out executions in the meantime.

"It's like a surgeon saying, 'We're not sure whether a lobotomy is going to work or not, we're studying it, but we're going to go through with it anyway,'" said Bill Breeden, who is wearing a cowboy hat and clutching a white cardboard placard with "Abolish the Death Penalty" printed in black marker.

They have tried logic. Now they turn to prayer. As 1 a.m. nears, they light red candles shielded by paper cups and gather in a circle. Breeden, Unitarian minister and folk singer and country boy from O'Bannon's southern Indiana, leads the invocation of Bivins; of his victim, the Reverend William Radcliffe; of the condemned man's mother and the victim's widow.

They sing:

Peace is flowing like a river,
flowing out from you and me,
flowing out into the desert,
setting all the captives free.

A single car horn sounds. The state and national flags snap in the bitter wind atop a pole behind the preacher.

Kafoure says he does not feel good about living under either of those flags tonight. Michael Hartt counters that there is justice to be found in the state and the nation, but it is in their constitutions, and callow politicians must be made to enforce them.

Lingle speaks of the human cost of answering violence with violence. "I think of Gerald Bivins's family," she said. "Being a mother, I can't imagine what it's like to be his mother right now."

Several others among the ten men and five women have a say, and then it is 1:30 a.m., and Bivins is presumed to be dead.

Breeden thanks "the people who stand in the dark and the cold honoring the dignity of life."

He voices the thin hope that "we don't have to do this many more times."

Under the streetlights and a cloud-smudged moon on this lovely stretch of the urban good life, rumpled signs are collected and hauled away till next time.

McVeigh, Breaking or Making?

MAY 2, 2001

How can we give Timothy McVeigh exactly what he desires and claim he is getting exactly what he deserves?

It is a simple question that we have chosen to answer not with thought but with brutality, much as McVeigh used mass murder to respond to a government he judged guilty of murder.

On May 16 the government will complete the ascent of this towering loser by descending to his level. He will have the satisfaction of knowing the survivors of his victims watched him go, leaving them no more chance to haunt him as he always will haunt them.

They can hope he repents at agonizing leisure in the afterlife; but an afterlife implies a God who, in the minds of many of us, reserves vengeance to Himself and forbids us to wish any sinner, even a cocksure killer of children, eternal fire.

Theologies do battle when capital punishment arises. There is debate within and among the major faiths as to the circumstances under which Scripture allows the state to take a life. But it's probably safe to say most Americans don't fall back on their religion in giving the thumbs-up or thumbs-down.

The Roman Catholic Church officially, and Indianapolis Archbishop Daniel Buechlein personally, oppose the death penalty in all cases. But polls show the majority of Catholics favor it. Moreover, the liberal Catholics who oppose it are not always comfortable with the church's persistent linking of capital punishment and abortion; while conservative Catholics are irritated to see men on Death Row raised to the level of unborn innocents.

To the latter, opponents of capital punishment would answer: Blame the state. By moving to deprive someone of life, it distills him down to the core of his humanity, his immortal soul.

Since most of us in the body politic do not ponder this reality, we tend to go by a rough system of weights and measures. Did the guy perpetrate a deed horrible enough, and react to it coldly enough, that merely losing his freedom will not balance the scales?

It can be an atrocity with a single victim, if the helplessness and the cruelty tear our hearts and defy our comprehension. It can be an offense with no actual victims, say, the trading of atomic secrets with an enemy.

Or it can be Oklahoma City. It can be a number so great, with the innocence of the victims so profound, and remorse so far from the murderer's consciousness, that we do not feel we need to look for a line that was crossed. We only need ask: If not McVeigh, then for God's sake, who?

In the cries of the dead and the pleas of their families, we think we hear the answer clearly. But we are asking the wrong question.

This is not about McVeigh. This is about us. We are free to choose whether to take a human life. We are free to choose, as has most of the so-called developed world, not to take life as a criminal penalty. Our choice should not depend on the choice someone else made, least of all this least of men.

McVeigh, child of God, is a gold-plated bum. Still in his twenties, he found his life shrunken to three possible accomplishments: violence, fame, and veneration by the brotherhood of aggrieved white American males.

He made it, Ma, as Cagney would say. Top of the burning world.

Even as they denounce his insane act, elements of the paranoid right blame the government for setting him off by taking on insurrectionists who were holed up with guns. Janet Reno's the devil, and she done made him do it.

Where were these voices when Black Panthers were murdered in their beds by police in the 1960s? And whose turn is it, the right or the left, to bomb the next classroom or day-care center to get back at the Federal Bureau of Investigation or the United Nations?

McVeigh is a small man who has been made a big deal by rapacious news media and a nasty political climate. His execution has editors and assorted loonies salivating. It will turn Terre Haute into a wired version of Caligula's Rome. And it will be televised—to victims' families, who know no more than we how they'll be affected, and maybe to the world, if hackers seize this irresistible opportunity.

It will be McVeigh Day, a holy day of obligation for crackpots and the fulfillment of this infanticidal fool's misbegotten mission.

It does not, or did not, have to be that way. It should be just one more unmarked day in a long, long confrontation between a human being who played God and the truth he wants his fellow mortals to help him escape.

Peace Monument? There's a Battle

MAY 8, 2002

Blessed are the peacemakers, but honored they are not.

Not officially. Not in Indiana, not popularly, not in stone and not in statesmen's speeches.

Many are the monuments and ceremonies around our city and state exalting those who have taken up arms at the behest of government. This month especially will see a heavy dose of tribute paid to military endeavor, generally taken to be the purest expression of patriotism.

We have Memorial Day coming, we have the Crusade to Crush Evil still running, we have the refurbished Indiana War Memorial, we have the sculptures marking the Vietnam and Korean wars and feting the crew of the USS *Indianapolis*. We even have the hundredth anniversary of the Soldiers and Sailors Monument. Millions of dollars have gone into these structures, and millions of deaths shadow them—deaths of enlistees and draftees and professionals; deaths of noncombatants, such as the hundreds of thousands at Tokyo and Hiroshima and Nagasaki, who found themselves under the wrong flag at the wrong time.

The sanctified space, and for the most part the speeches, do not accommodate the civilian casualties or the enemy-of-the-moment soldiers. Even Maya Lin's haunting Vietnam Veterans Memorial in Washington, D.C., the most antiwar of any government-commissioned war monument, lists only some fifty thousand dead—the Americans, who comprise a fraction of the total lives taken in a futile campaign to subdue a faraway sliver of land that's since become a trading partner.

The waste of war, the full price it exacts and the disdain it ultimately shows for any nation's colors or ideology, are not the business of monuments and orators. They reserve their application of duty, honor, and sacrifice to those who donned a certain uniform and went where they were sent. It is because of them, we say, that we have peace. In a democracy, is that all we can say about the role of the citizen in matters of government resort to force?

How about a monument, in this city that devotes so much granite and marble and limestone to members of the armed forces, to those who served by trying to keep us out of war?

The Charles Litekys, Muriel Rukeysers, Albert Einsteins, George McGoverns, Thomas Gumbletons, and Jody Williamses. At home, the likes of Ron and Jane Haldeman, Bill and Glenda Breeden, JoAnne Lingle, and Eugene Debs. The innumerable and mostly invisible ranks of religious witnesses, atheistic idealists, serious-minded celebrities, independent-minded politicians, picket-walking grandparents, fed-up combat veterans, and others who have resisted the big-stick approach to foreign policy that the United States has chosen more than two hundred times in its history.

Enlistees and never draftees, they have worked, sacrificed, risked, lost, served jail time, taken beatings, even gotten killed for the same cause—life and liberty—that supposedly gives the military its purpose. Yet their inclusion in a Memorial Day gala would be unthinkable.

There are plenty of monuments to peace, of course, but they tend to be private affairs. This makes sense inasmuch as peacemaking tends to place one in opposition to government. Moreover, the peace movement by nature is global, and public officials get chilly toward anything that will not fit under one flag.

Take the Reverend Martin Luther King Jr. At a time when he lived in justified fear for his own safety, he was awarded the Nobel Peace Prize on an international stage. Some years after his death, his birth anniversary was made a national holiday; but rarely does his opposition to the Vietnam War intrude upon the platitudes that politicians purvey in those January rituals.

"We sterilize our martyrs," observed Ken Brown, director of the Peace Studies Institute at Manchester College. "But the three themes we need to remember regarding Dr. King were economic injustice, racism and militarism."

Must we trouble ourselves with such messiness when we're designing monuments and drafting speeches?

"I think we should," Brown said. "It's what we need most. True patriotism argues against destructive policies."

Terrific. Now let's see about getting that national peace park appropriation added to the Patriot Act.

Muffled Drumbeat

JANUARY 15, 2003

Safely dead, the Reverend Martin Luther King Jr. will be praised in the coming days by all manner of politicians and pundits who may or may not be taking time out from their normal business of promoting tax breaks for Wall Street, abolishment of affirmative action, and war in Iraq.

The ripoff of a great American revolutionary by defenders of the rigged system he challenged is possible because so few of us know what he stood for and so many consider his holiday no more than a bone thrown to a whiny minority in the first place.

So here's Martin the Dreamer, conjured up for the annual seance in which black hand clutches white hand and everybody congratulates himself for not being prejudiced, as if that's all there were to racism.

Would King be part of the ceremonies if he were to return today, the seventy-fourth anniversary of his birth, or this holiday weekend? Maybe. He was a conciliator of the sort sorely needed in today's political climate.

I like to think, however, that he would be somewhere most of the wielders of power will not be.

Last Friday, the preacher who was killed on a mission to help Memphis sanitation workers might have been at our own City-County Building, where the Community Faith and Labor Coalition celebrated modest raises received by our lowest-paid municipal employees and vowed to continue striving for a "living wage" ordinance, adopted by more than a hundred other cities.

This Saturday, no doubt, he would be in Washington, D.C., or San Francisco, or downtown Indianapolis, where hundreds of thousands will demonstrate against the next attack on the destitute subjects of Saddam Hussein.

Joining the world community in opposition to President George W. Bush's war is a sure way to be branded un-American, a charge that was hurled at King when he challenged a liberal government over Vietnam. The connection he made between injustice in Mississippi and suffering abroad bespoke a level of prophecy to which mere reformers, including most of his fellow churchmen, were not ready to rise.

To King, taking sides against "the shirtless and barefoot people of the land" was itself un-American, especially since our poor would do the dirty work. When he counseled poor Americans to embrace nonviolence, "They asked if our own nation wasn't using massive doses of violence to solve its problems, to bring about the changes it wanted. Their questions hit home, and I knew that I could never again raise my voice against the violence of the oppressed in the ghettos without having first spoken clearly to the greatest purveyor of violence in the world today—my own government."

In his speech before a church assembly in New York City in 1967, King pleaded for an end to the madness of us versus them and ours versus theirs. A generation later, as American troops mass in the Middle East, American dissenters mass in many cities, and American consumers amass their goods, his words ring out with eerie clarity: "I am convinced that if we are to get on the right side of the world revolution, we as a nation must undergo a radical revolution of values. We must rapidly begin the shift from a 'thing-oriented' society to a 'person-oriented' society. When machines and computers, profit motives and property rights are considered more important than people, the giant triplets of racism, materialism and militarism are incapable of being conquered."

That's applied religion. You can only dream of finding it at your local MLK festivities.

Givin' 'em the Dickens

DECEMBER 25, 2002

The snow-framed sign over the ponderous oaken doors read "Bowen, Bayh, O'Bannon, Borst, Bauer, Bosma and Scroosier," but only the last of these quarrelsome old partners, the fearsome wizened Ebenezer, was still around to answer the tired tinkle that announced visitors.

"Please do come in, gentlemen!" the proprietor growled. "Scratchoff, help our guests with their coats. We do want them to feel at home, don't we? And what may we help you with this blustery evening? Campaign contribution envelopes? Lobbyist registration forms? Tea?"

As the harried assistant Bob Scratchoff scrambled to collect their furs, the most distinguished of the three men stepped forward and cleared his throat.

"Well, actually, Mr. Scroosier, we've not come to make a donation, but to ask for one."

Ebenezer dropped his quill and glared over his pince-nez.

"I beg your pardon!"

"It is that time of the year, Mr. Scroosier. It is giving time. It is Session Season."

"The Session! Bah! Nothing but an excuse to get into a man's pocket every 12 months."

"Ah, but sir, there are a great many who have given of themselves to your enterprise throughout the year and now find themselves in need. Manufacturers. Utilities. Casinos. Tax lawyers. They sometimes seem beyond number to us, who devote ourselves to their representation."

"Perhaps, then, it's time to reduce the surplus population!"

"As it happens, both the surplus and the population are in reduction. Those in the population who graduate from college tend to depart to get work. It's called the, er, brain drain, sir."

"Departing? Are there no workhouses here?"

"Oh, some very large ones, Mr. Scroosier. They fall under the heading of Department of Correction. Quite a thriving enterprise. But most expensive. It also needs your assistance."

Ebenezer sat back from his ledgers with hands behind his head and regarded the visitors with a leer.

"You know, gentlemen, I had a premonition you'd be darkening my door, silk hats in hand. Last night, in what I thought was a terrible nightmare (that ham and cheese from the Press Club), all my long-dead partners came clanking through my bedroom with their budget surpluses chained to them, and they warned me to change my miserly ways. They threatened to keep sending more ghosts until I was shamed and terrified into flinging tax money out the window at orphans and invalids."

A younger member of the delegation broke in. "I must say, that's a very moving story, sir. How did it end?"

"It ended," Ebenezer snarled, "when I ordered the whole bunch of them off the premises and vowed to take care of the needy as we've always done. And that gentlemen, is where you come in. Scratchoff, escort our fine fellows to the vault and have them serve themselves."

The senior visitor spoke again, his voice choked.

"Why, thank you, sir. We truly are touched by your generosity in these difficult times. Frankly, we feared our rather resplendent appearance might put you off."

"You are a posh lot, it's true, but I'm comfortable with that."

"All the same, sir, we did bring Scratchoff's stepchild, Tiny Trim, along for variety's sake. Poor little fellow just couldn't quite negotiate the steps in this snow with that broken cane. Shall we fetch him?"

"Let's wait till spring," Ebenezer replied. "Savings must come from somewhere, and there's always pain. Scratchoff, go wish your kid a Merry Session from us all, and tell him hey, have a nice night."

Double, Double, Toil, Trouble

JULY 3, 2005

Those witches could have saved Macbeth and Company a load of grief if their ability to see down the road had been properly credited. So could today's naysayers, scraggly and otherwise, if the Daniels administration would only stop seeing double.

Double the livestock production from factory farming, that already hoggish befouler of air and menace to water and soil.

Double the cost of extending I-69 from Indianapolis to Evansville by sticking with the messiest of possible routes.

Environmental protection got scant attention from either Daniels or then-Governor Joe Kernan during the 2004 election campaign. But economic development, which continues to be treated as somehow free of the Earth, did play a starring role. Big farming and the biggest possible I-69, budgetwise and landscapewise, are the horses the governor is riding; and the dump they will take will be an ecological statement and legacy.

Ecology, let's remember, is a broad concept, extending not just to brown bats and old trees but to the human communities that live off the same air, water, and sunlight. Some of these folks still live in the country, and they object to breathing essence of offal from pig plants that spew as much waste as a city.

Nor is moving to the city any escape. Manure spills from these sprawling meat mills are commonplace, and the bacteriological effects on both ground and surface water cannot be fully measured or contained, much as the government and the proprietors urge our trust in their technology and will.

Double it? That's not only dangerous, it's defeatist. It implies that dispersed family farming on a smaller-than-industrial scale cannot succeed. That's not true; and it would prove even more dramatically untrue if the megafarms had to bear the full cost of their rear-end output. It smacks of neocolonialism that Dutch agribusinessmen chafing under Europe's protectiveness toward rural culture are exhorted to go West, young man, and have at the American Heartland.

Bigger costs more, and the cost is not just in dollars but in quality of life. In the case of I-69, ecology and economy alike are being defied in dogged pursuit of the costliest and most difficult path, the one that plows through forests and farms rather than adapting existing highways. As if it were a revelation, the Daniels administration now tells us there's not enough money for I-69 and the long list of other road additions and repairs; so wait an extra ten years and blame the Democrats, but by no means look for the exit.

Nor stop spending. Daniels, who expressed reasonable doubt about the "new-terrain" route for I-69 early in his election campaign, has since buckled in for the long ride into the misty future and OK'd the multimillion-dollar dribble of planning funds while the actual construction of the boondoggle awaits more urgent road projects.

From the national level to struggling towns throughout southwest Indiana, we are told, I-69 is vital to economic viability. Yet we've had a decade of the North American Free Trade Agreement without the so-called NAFTA highway, and we've got more interstate density in this economically depressed state than almost anywhere else.

That's double reason to build it for half price, if you must build it. And do not go whole hog with the savings.

Give an ear to the witches. They may not be your people, but hold your nose and look deeper into the caldron. It may turn you around.

Songs for the Road

Drawing a deep breath and laying down the sword, or sawed-off pool cue, for the moment, the devotee of the journalism of wrath reflects with sadness, hope, affection, and laughter on the relentless life that has made his living. The meditations might rest on a personal passage—a solemn rite of pitch and catch with a homegrown Little Leaguer or an unrequited love affair with a derelict "classic" car—or take flight to the length and breadth of a dear disappointing state and the ends of an imperiled, impossibly lovable planet. The tone may shift 180 degrees from giving politicians pointers on courting the archetypal Hoosier voter to seeking solace in elusive silence on the anniversary of a national tragedy, but it is all of a spiritual piece, a chorus joined in a profession of defiant faith.

One Year Later

SEPTEMBER 11, 2002

It is too bad this cannot be a day of silence.

Not a moment. Not a pause. Not a brisk ritual of hat removal and hand clasping before engines and televisions and ungoverned throats resume their idiot's sound and fury.

Not a stolen respite from an onslaught of specials and speeches and posturing and promotions that would propose to honor the voiceless with monuments of noise.

Not a typical festive free-market day, extraordinary only for the size of its ordinariness and the volume of its shrillness.

No. A day apart.

A day fully and untouchably its own, as that one was, and is, in spite of all the claims we have made upon it.

A day for them.

No pontificating, no saber rattling, no blame placing, no huckstering, no rhapsodizing, no sermonizing, no demonizing.

No praying. No weeping.

No business as usual.

For that is what we have done. Ever since the first few of us uttered the first "Oh my Gods" and called our loved ones and coworkers to the television.

Incapable of comprehending the calculated deaths of thousands—incinerated, hurtled, crushed, entombed in mountains of rubble, sacrificed to madness as they went about their morning of sales meetings and coffee breaks and singsong instructions from flight attendants—we commenced immediately to weave what we wanted around the event and move on, avoiding its gaze.

We called it anything and everything. A Pearl Harbor. A divine judgment. A blow against liberalism or imperialism or isolationism or democracy. A crucible for heroism. A forge for a new American solidarity. A call to love. An excuse to hate.

We made it an opportunity. A commodity. A cliché.

There were valid reasons for elected officials and journalists and child psychologists and entertainers and members of countless other interest groups to fold that day into their repertoire. And each in his or her own way, usually without malicious intent, misused it.

It was not on behalf of those three thousand that Afghanistan was bombed, or a change in immigration policy was demanded, or due process was suspended, or professional experts went on television to reassure parents, or ballplayers went on with their games wearing FDNY caps.

It was not out of anguish for the dead that the media told us we were shopping more to lift our spirits, or choosing soothing colors in our home decor, or bringing back those daring Stars and Stripes casual fashions.

We care, but we all have our agendas—bleeding-heart liberal pundits as much as anyone. Those deaths that day came at the hands of people who very probably did not follow the parlor debate over Republican versus Democrat foreign policy. Yet the debate drones on, muffling the screams.

Have we learned anything from the day we know so casually by a number? Have we grown, or diminished? I look around at those of us who only witnessed the horror from afar, and did not feel the cold grip of personal loss, and I see the same roaring, brassy, narcissistic gang I knew and loved on September 10, 2001.

I need to see the ones we have lost. I need to hear them. I need to find a way to give this day to them alone.

I need a day of silence. I know I could begin by being part of it. I could spare you all this pomposity. But I have to make a living. You understand.

The Risen, the Fallen, the Choice

APRIL 20, 2003

In his immortal poem "Easter, 1916," William Butler Yeats wrote lines for Ireland that would serve as an epitaph for many a tragic people:

Too long a sacrifice
Can make a stone of the heart.

The very stones underfoot spoke of the sacrifice of his time and place. Battered in spirit, physically hungry, treated as undesirables in their own land by a superior power proclaiming a superior religion, the Irish of Yeats's inspiration rose up on the Christian feast of triumph not in hope of glory but out of nothing to lose.

Hearts hardened by earthly reality, they mocked the Resurrection and were mocked by it in turn, though their crushing defeat did prove a symbolic breakthrough toward independence.

Too long a sacrifice, and still being demanded, in Northern Ireland and so many other Irelands. Still exacted in besieged towns and refugee camps and smoking rubble around the world. Still nagging and still clawing at our cuffs as we in the comfortable minority bask in our radiant rite of spring.

No doubt many of our services today will be sweetened with an air of self-congratulation, our prayers having been answered with destruction of the infidel, our purpose and preeminence in God's sight reaffirmed.

"I am your God. You are my people," went the Old Testament reading one Sunday during a Lent that coincided almost exactly with another war. It was not a comforting message to me on this latest of the countless occasions on which I have heard it. If religion truly is to be taken as the ultimate sorting of the tribes, no wonder we have regular news stories of gunfire "marring" holy days at sacred sites.

On this Easter Sunday, we find two of the West's great religions at war with the third. As an Irish American Catholic drawing from personal memory as well as historical awareness, I am grateful neither front is united. Voices of reconciliation vie with cries for retribution. Prayers are said, even from the highest pulpits, for all of war's victims and not just its victors.

Prayers for peace rise from our safe churches as well as from battlefields and bombed cities. But history affords these petitions little support. The big picture, to use the military strategists' jargon, looks like one continuous ten thousand-year conflict, a Picasso *Guernica* of anguish feeding into anguish. All the religions teach that peace comes not from political institutions but from individual hearts, yet politics keeps demanding its sacrifices and soft hearts can bear up only so long.

People in some of the world's most destitute, disease-ridden, and oppressed communities amaze visitors with their hospitality and love of life. When they fight back against their plight, it is often nonviolent but often not; sometimes, acts of pure vengeance erupt from the pressure of sacrifice imposed upon them.

Here in my world, where so little sacrifice is asked, the heart is free to remain vulnerable to suffering and to nag and claw against complacency and complicity. But there is a cost to that. The late peace activist Philip Berrigan said that if he could not change the government, at least the government would not change him. But political events do change us—they trouble our sleep, wrack us with anger, and steal our hope.

As participants in a divided democracy, we find ourselves in a verbal brawl rather than a civic conversation, and we are sorely tempted to just quit the fray, a privilege not available to most of humanity. Because we know their sacrifice, we are obliged not to turn our eyes away, our hearts to stone.

Farewell My Ugly (Apologies to E. B. White)
APRIL 2, 1997

All these lamentations over changing our archaic high school basketball tournament put me in mind of a story about nostalgia.

It was not exactly my dream car (a Volkswagen Beetle), but it was close enough (a 1963 Corvair), and when I heard the rasp of its air-cooled engine and the plaintive ah-OOH-gah of its horn on that fine spring afternoon a couple years ago, I skipped to the curb like the kid I proposed to become.

My wife, on the other hand, refused to come out of the house, even though the friend who was lending me this squat, stick shifting, quasi classic was a friend of hers, too.

He remains her friend, thanks to my ultimate decision not to take him up on his offer to return me to my high school days for a flat five hundred dollars.

Unlike myself, my friend has purchased, on an ordinary middle-class income, the fondly remembered and technologically primitive rear-driven cars that I might purchase if I were to win the lottery. He has had dozens of them, not because he loves them but because he likes them, and he does not doctor them along when death draws near.

"If you wrap it around a tree," he told me, "just call me, and I'll come pick it up."

Thus dispensed, I yanked open the creaking door and descended into the driver's seat, where my arranged love affair encountered its first crisis: I found out what the floor in a very old Chevy without a carpet looks like.

Because beauty's only skin deep, and because I could not see deeper than this particular skin (i.e., to the pavement), I forgave the flaw and started 'er up. This could be accomplished without use of a key, another opportunity to look on the positive side when a cynic might fret about, say, security.

The report of that vacuum-cleaner motor was just as I remembered it, but the four on the floor was, as my friend had warned, "a little stiff."

After about three blocks, my shoulder felt as if I had just thrown fifty fastballs. This was supposed to be fun.

The fun, I decided, would not be in the driving but in the being seen driving. People just have to notice a Corvair.

"How old is that?" a guy at the Shell station asked. "It's a '63," I smugly replied. He stared a moment and turned back to pumping gas into his taller, larger car. He did not offer to swap.

My teenage son liked the Corvair, though not necessarily on terms set by the car or by me. He took to hurling himself against the seat in gleeful rhythm with my somewhat convulsive gear shifting. When I offered him a special treat, a lift to school, he replied cheerfully but prohibitively, "That's OK."

Sometimes romance takes a little imagination. When my wife finally took her seat in this coach of reverie, she pointed to the floor.

"That's rust."

"Well, yes, but it's not really rusted through to the bottom."

"That's the floor."

"Well, yes . . ."

"That's the bottom."

When I called my friend after a couple weeks and bade him pick up his little car, I did not use family disapproval as an alibi. I myself had discovered a truth and I faced it: With old cars, as with old sports traditions, there are a few who honestly like them, a great many who will not even look up when they go by, and a legion who love them only as long as they are dreams.

My Golden Age
JANUARY 4, 1998

Maybe it was William Faulkner who said the past is never really past.

Maybe it was not Faulkner. Maybe it was Peter Cushing, who had the title role in *The Curse of Frankenstein.*

Certainly, the idea that there's no escaping one's history was brought home to me more forcefully in the moralistic horror movies of the early Technicolor epoch than in any classroom or library.

And certainly the cyclic nature of life—unquenchable by a thousand deaths—is demonstrated in the building on the near south side where I shuddered through those B movies.

Recent news of the bowling alley that has opened in the Fountain Square Building, joining the 1950s-style diner and other enterprises that already had started the revival there, cast me back to days that are half buried like gold nuggets and land mines in my consciousness.

To appreciate the reborn Fountain Square Building, and the disinterred Fountain Square Theater that once was its centerpiece, you have to remember, or imagine, the Indianapolis of the premall, presprawl, preslasher flick era, when neighborhoods were bricks in the city's wall and not just pretty balloons in political speeches.

To a young person in that smaller world, the five-story brown commercial fortress was truly awesome—a block long chunk of downtown looming over the taverns and shoe stores of Shelby Street.

Doctors and dentists had their offices there, as they had them downtown before the exodus to Eighty-sixth Street. I would take the elevator (run by a lady with a crank) to the marbled upper floors, where the view of skeletal black-iron fire escapes prepared me for the laughing gas and pliers that were the short answer to toothaches for folks with short money.

Today, you can still have a human elevator operator take you upstairs, where a different kind of visual punch awaits in the form of unabashed artwork by people who are HIV-positive. HIV/AIDS was unheard of when the doctors were there, but still, there's a continuum between Heart Rays, the arts agency, and its predecessors, in filling basic needs for people of modest means.

Where modesty stopped, in the building's previous life, was at the marquee-hooded entryway to the Fountain Square Theater, one of those pharaonic monuments to Hollywood's golden age that are sinking beneath urban deserts all over America.

In a time when sneakers were two dollars a pair and were not replaced until their soles were flapping, we watched *Attack of the Crab Monsters* and *The Ten Commandments* from plush seats below towering brocaded ceilings set with frosted lights and giant urns.

We blew corn kernels through soda straws onto the crowd from the concealing gloom of a genuine balcony. We shouted commands from the throne-like stuffed chairs of a smoking lounge fit for Cushing's baronial mansion.

All this for a quarter a double feature, cartoons included. No commercials, no beseechments to keep quiet and refrain from smoking during the show.

In the heady heyday of the Fountain, ushers with flashlights kicked you out when you acted up. They are old men now, or dead, but they are still swaggering and fearsome in my memory. Like Cushing and his dreaded creation. Like the outsized building and its life-and-death businesses.

Resurrected but never really dead. Open for revisiting, but never really departed from.

Urban Renewal Squared
JUNE 15, 2011

I have friends who have moved into a couple of houses on Hosbrook Street in my old Fountain Square neighborhood, a happening place but a long way from Lockerbie when it comes to cachet value of venerable fixer-uppers.

What's remarkable to me about these homesteaders is something that rather dates me. They are white.

As a grade-schooler, I carried newspapers on Hosbrook Street, virtually the only two blocks where African Americans resided in that blue-collar enclave. An island, or more accurately isthmus, of diversity in a pre-Great Society community where Negroes were foreign and feared. It was not really diversity at all, in other words, but rather, a cameo branch of segregation in a city where generations lived and died with Balkanization and with a superficially benign aristocracy that did not allow much room under the tent for Irish, Italians, Jews, Kentuckians, and other shirttail relatives.

We had no clue what history and the powers that be had done to divide us up, but we did our part. The Protestants called us "catlickers," we Irish Catholics struck sparks with the Italian Catholics, and the stereotypes about Jews and blacks rolled along in breezy defiance of the truth we should have learned from meeting them, opening books, and following the news. Jews and blacks knew which swimming clubs they could patronize. Gay still meant happy; homosexuals had no permission to be happy, and Ali was about all we knew about Muhammad.

By the late 1960s, Negroes were black, the ghettoization of their neighborhoods and schools had been exposed and outlawed in Indianapolis as in the South, and their neighborhood and mine had been lacerated by an equal opportunity freeway system sacrificing all of us to the convenience of suburban commuters. Not that interracial solidarity automatically ensued therefrom, but forces were hard at work to remake the place where everyone knew his and her place.

Last weekend, as I waded through bodies of every description at the Italian Street Festival in the remnant of the old Holy Rosary Catholic Church neighborhood, I nearly laughed out loud at the change I have lived to witness in the city of my birth and the continuing dogged resistance.

Imagine. That same day, a Gay Pride Parade, complete with politicians, corporate vendors, and even cops marching in uniform. With "family" advocates duly appalled and warning us of doom at the hands of "activist judges," the same label conservatives of forty years ago slapped on those who issued busing orders.

Imagine. Spanish in the air in Fountain Square, soaring amid the political flak, above the cries for English only. A Muslim representing the old neighborhood in Congress. Artists' space in the old G. C. Murphy Company, a department store so big in my youth it could save you from a trip downtown, where who knows what sort of people you might run into.

Mock Heroics

MARCH 2, 2001

Years ago in an interview, I asked Michael Jordan whether he thought mass-marketed media figures such as he were afforded exaggerated stature in our society.

Sure they are, he replied. But consider the alternative.

"What do you do to change it?" Jordan asked. "It's a trend that's been going on, and I think you've got a lot of kids who don't have any other role models to look at. They look at entertainers and athletes as something that's very positive, the way they want to be."

Setting aside the credibility questions raised by Jordan's off-court career as a capitalist carnival barker, his remarks are well worth weighing.

Kids have always filled their dreams with ballplayers and movie stars; and today's dreamers include many fatherless youngsters who rely upon the Jordans and the rappers to plug holes in their reality.

Better the hero on television than the hero on the street corner, the thinking goes.

Yet the fundamental basis for the attraction is not altogether different. And the worship of pop-culture gods is hardly just kid stuff.

Like the drug dealer from the neighborhood, the boxer and the singer and the sports star typically are poor-to-working-class scrappers who have broken through to material success and flaunt it in front of those who would be their bosses.

Tailored Joe Louis waving from touring cars paid for by fallen White Hopes.

Orphaned Babe Ruth drawing a bigger paycheck than the president and saying why not, he had a better year.

Michael Jackson from Gary, Frank Sinatra from Hoboken, Joe DiMaggio from the waterfront of San Francisco.

Dale Earnhardt Sr. from Kannapolis, North Carolina, dropping out of high school to drive jalopy racers and going on to become a deified multimillionaire.

Say what you will about the intangible appeal of these men, without having made it, in a material sense, they would not be known far and wide as heroes.

Money is an indispensable measure of this sort of greatness, and on the face of it, nothing could be more juvenile. Pete Rose, who was the most delightful of baseball players but the most stunted of personalities, summed up his philosophy of life when he said he did not care how much he was paid as long as it was more than anyone else in the game. His dignity depended on that.

The immaturity of using money and fame as standards of value ought to imply that we had grown out of our idolatry toward these warriors without a war. But it was not children who were figuratively hurling themselves onto Earnhardt's funeral pyre a few days ago.

One of the most disliked men in racing, as well as one of the most admired, The Intimidator was praised after his death as a wonderful husband, father, and friend. That all may be true, but it's not why millions of strangers loved him and arranged their lives to follow his parade.

Winners become heroes because they win. Once they become heroes, we begin to ascribe virtues to them that true archetypal heroes would have: compassion, civic concern, devotion to family, and willingness to sacrifice. Indeed, these also are traits ordinary people are supposed to cultivate, but the pro football player who unloads food baskets from his Lexus once a year is much more interesting to us than the seventy-year-old lady who rides the 6 a.m. bus to her volunteer job at the soup kitchen.

As we build bedroom shrines to race drivers and laud rock stars for making hospital visits, truly heroic and saintly acts are being performed all around us every day. If we would wipe our eyes of the stage tears, we might see that it is titillation and triumph we are really looking for in our objects of devotion.

"It's just like when Elvis died," a fan said on the radio as he pondered life without Dale Earnhardt.

So much for America's loss of childish innocence. Joltin' Joe, gone away? From this game? It ain't gonna be so, kid.

Your Kid: Champ or Chump?

AUGUST 31, 2001

A friend of mine who was quite devoted to the local high school football team (he taught at the school, his son played in the line), was moved at one point to complain to the coach about the length of practices, which were exhausting the players and cutting into homework time.

We have got to do this if we want to win, the coach explained to him.

Well, my friend said, then lose.

By the professed principles of youth sports in America, there is nothing radical about that reply.

We play for fun, for camaraderie, for physical fitness, for self-improvement, for enhancement of the education experience, and for the filling of that dangerous idle time. Winning, though nice, is certainly not essential to the brief golden moment in our lives when we take our turn at athletics.

Yeah.

Right.

While a great many young wearers of numbered shirts, and their families, can indeed take or leave winning and losing, and can take or leave sports altogether for that matter, the inescapable fact is that solemn competition on the field and court has grown into both industry and religion in this society, with success and failure clearly and simply defined.

We do not have tyke soccer programs because kids need a chance to play together. We do not have a Little League World Series on television because miniature baseball is cute. We do not have facilities at Disney World for amateur basketball tournaments to promote fellowship between teenagers from various states.

We do not push the Indiana High School Athletic Association to drop its ban on summer coaching because football players cannot get enough of those delightful August two-a-day practices.

We get our kids involved in organized sports sooner, longer, more intensely, more expensively, more exclusively, more politically, more angrily, more litigiously, and more ludicrously than ever before because parents want to win.

Not just games. Goodies.

Prestige. Publicity. Roster spots on elite teams. Compliments from clinic directors. Attention from high school coaches. Scholarships from college coaches. Admiration—bag that, how about envy—from other parents.

If you move in these circles, you know the Pompon Parent lexicon. All-stars. Travel team. AAU. Summer league. Winter conditioning. Division I.

Division I, as in scholarship to a major college, serves as both the Holy Grail to fanatical sports parents and the cover for their embarrassment at being fanatics. We would not be pushing our kid, in other words, if it were not for the practical reality of needing money for school.

This is, in the vast majority of cases, disingenuous. The child a) has no prospect of winning an athletic scholarship, b) will find his or her way to college anyway, like the rest of us, and/or c) will have enough parental money spent on team dues and travel to invest in a certificate of deposit that would cover Harvard.

Pelé became a soccer star by kicking a wad of rags through the streets. His pint-size heir in North America, 2001, lives like a star already, escorted to manicured fields with Dad as chauffeur and Mom to bear the cooler and the bag of balls.

Parents of a local Little League team were cited in the paper recently as having maxed out their credit cards to support their children's crusade for glory. This was portrayed as noble sacrifice, à la immigrant dishwashers scrimping for their children's schooling, when it looked a lot like plain old middle-class excess. I mean, do kids really need national championships? And if national championships are so special, how come there are so darn many of them?

I would hate to give the impression I condemn these folks. I sympathize. If they do not haul their youngsters all over the landscape in pursuit of their dreams, other parents will. And other children will win. And where some children are winners, other children must be losers, and their parents must bear the pain.

Boomers: Feeling Busted
MARCH 20, 2002

I suppose we have ourselves to blame, those of us who ganged up and got born between World War II and Vietnam, the period known for better, and for steadily worse, as the baby boom.

We were the five hundred-pound gorilla cohort, the force behind history's greatest economic expansion, the slashing horde of global pop culture.

We wanted everything—to own the world, to change the world, to go boldly forth seeking other worlds—and we had no intention of sharing credit with the bald and the boring.

Talkin' 'bout my g-g-g-generation.
Hope I die before I get o-o-o-old.

We may not have started youth worship, but we wrote the missals and built the basilicas (with entrepreneurs of all ages eagerly passing the collection baskets). We thought we were smarter and more noble, not just cooler, than our elders. "Kids" carried the same cachet in the 1960s that "working families" commanded for Al Gore in 2000. You know, as in, "We don't care how crowded the chancellor's calendar is, we've got some kids here who deserve some answers!"

Heady days, those. For those who lived them, that is.

The problem with characterizing a generation, especially the most populous of generations, is that there is no such thing as a typical experience. Moreover, some of the most atypical phenomena may be the best remembered and most readily associated because they were conspicuous.

Woodstock? The Weathermen? Free love? LSD? Come on. One south-side workingman's bar went through more chemicals in the 1960s than all the college kids in Indianapolis. A black militant got elected student body president at Indiana University back then, but so did a Young Republican.

"I missed the '60s," a long-haired columnist for the old *Milwaukee Journal*, who happened to be a Purdue University alumnus, retorted one time in the 1970s when he was accused of being a 1960s radical. "I spent them in Indiana."

Much of America would have left him with the same deprivation. The age of the baby boomers' youth may have been a time of hedonistic experimentation and political upheaval, but no generation monopolized those developments and no generation was monopolized by them.

Yet, many of us chose to think otherwise. Now we are feeling the backlash.

In the rightward lurch the country's taken in recent years and especially recent months, the boomers have taken a tag team beating from those who contend we do not share the greatness of the World War II generation and will not share our goods with Generation X.

It is because of boomer greed that Social Security will be depleted before the Xers get to it. It is because of boomer depravity that the legacy of freedom left by our fallen troops is vulnerable to terrorists.

The most self centered of generations, a young pundit called us. His, he submitted, is the "cleanup generation," ready to help the Greatest Generation and the Bush administration deal with our mess.

Check your conservative, even some of your liberal, commentators. "Boomer" has become a pejorative.

Is it fair? Well, this peacenik generation left 50,000 lives in Vietnam, and like its fathers' generation, killed hundreds of thousands of enemies, many of them noncombatants. This generation also took to the streets and went to jail trying to stop its war, as did predecessors, who likewise faced the draft from which Gen Xers have been spared.

This generation gave lives in the Deep South for justice. This generation also threw rocks at civil rights demonstrators and could not have imagined a national holiday for their "drum major."

This generation grew up, got married, had children, sat in pews, checked investments, voted for Bush and voted for Gore. This generation gave us Neil Young and Rush Limbaugh.

When an acquaintance asked, with proper enthusiasm, whether I had read Tom Brokaw's *Greatest Generation*, I replied that I could not get past the premise—I did not believe you could rank huge collections of humans separated only by time. Harking to the Great Depression, the long, long war and the dreaded telegrams, he regarded me blankly. I was tempted to say every generation is as great as it has to be, but that would not have helped much. I had to live with the reality of perception, and the mess made by all this talkin' 'bout the high concepts of high-volume kids.

Prophets Doomed
JUNE 30, 2002

My father, I suppose, was about as sophisticated as your average working stiff, maybe even a bit more so. He knew a little William Shakespeare courtesy of the brothers at Cathedral High School and had seen a lot of Europe as a guest of Uncle Sam. He read the front of the newspaper before he turned to the sports.

He also faithfully read, and tirelessly and tiresomely cited, the daily column called "The Worry Clinic" by a small-town Indiana physician and psychologist named George W. Crane.

"It's like Dr. Crane says," Dad would intone. "Everybody has tattooed across his chest in invisible letters, I WANT TO BE IMPORTANT. If you treat them that way, you can't go wrong."

Such nuggets were no less profound than the advice for better living that's being retailed by "experts" on today's more colorful lifestyle pages. Far more urbane readers than my dad presumably are taking them as original wisdom.

The difference between then and now, I think, was not intellectual but emotional. Doctor Crane comforted readers. Knowing virtually nothing of his résumé, they gazed upon that thumbnail picture of the smiling sage in rimless spectacles and felt the presence of a breathing elder they could trust.

Years after my Crane-shadowed youth, I came to work for this newspaper and found myself sharing in the joke that was our grudging commitment to his column.

His wooden writing style, his antediluvian views on marriage, his shameless recycling of a handful of platitudes, everything about Doctor Crane drove professional journalists up the wall, and nothing but fear of loyalist rebellion kept him in the paper.

When "The Worry Clinic" finally, quietly, was dropped, in the early 1980s, no uproar ensued. No doubt, old age had silenced many of those voices. And clearly, the heyday of the newspaper columnist who could be embraced by the masses as part of the family had passed.

Eppie "Ann Landers" Lederer, who died a week ago, was, along with her sister Pauline "Dear Abby" Phillips, the most conspicuous survivor of the era of the homey print persona. Like Doctor Crane, Billy Graham, and Heloise Cruse (whose daughter keeps her homemaking column alive), she was an institution known on a first-name basis by legions of strangers seeking simple answers.

While the advice columns are far from dead, those first names do not resonate these days as, say, Oprah's and Rosie's do. Big-city newspapers have traded schmaltz for flash, and readers no longer sustain the illusion that a Doctor Crane—or an Erma Bombeck or a Mike Royko, working on a higher plane—is a neighbor stopping by for coffee with stories and an ear.

The sentimentality, blind faith, nostalgia, and bumper-sticker patriotism that characterized Ann Landers and her era remain alive in a more urbane and cynical America. But the majesty of newspapers and the innocence of readers that made a kindly aunt of a kitsch artist on deadline is gone with Joe DiMaggio. Eppie was right to insist her nom de plume be buried along with her.

We with Stars in Our Eyes
FEBRUARY 5, 2003

When the space shuttle *Challenger* exploded on the morning of January 28, 1986, I was burying my father in the south-side neighborhood where I grew up.

When *Discovery* was launched with bated breath on the morning of September 29, 1988, I was watching with my reporter's notebook from the steamy bank of the Banana River at Cape Canaveral.

When *Columbia* came apart over Texas last Saturday morning, I was running errands, oblivious to its existence.

Even then, I felt the tragedy personally, as should every human, not just every American and Israeli. And again, like most humans, I had no idea why those people were up there.

With *Challenger* and *Discovery*, the scientific and strategic importance of enormously expensive and far-from-routine ventures beyond the atmosphere never seemed to enter into my conversations, as a citizen or a journalist. There were other, more dramatic, concerns.

Challenger, with its smiling schoolteacher among the lost, brought a nation together in grief and prompted those of us who happened to have private grief at the time to ponder how small and how large the nonnewsworthy passages of our lives can be.

Discovery, the next try after thirty-two supposedly soul-searching, housecleaning months, brought us together in renewed romance, triumphantly marking its escape with a thin vapor trail across that blinding blue sky where its predecessor had dropped from a misshapen cloud of awful failure.

I remember interviewing fellow spectators about the tears—of joy, relief, pride, closure. This was not the America of 9/11, where you know the tiger of technology can maul you and leave you bleeding.

This was the land of Chuck Yeager and Tom Wolfe, still believing some cocky Yank in a crew cut will throw a saddle on the beast and y'all just relax, ma'am.

It is already clear, a few days after *Columbia*, that some public realism about the space program would have been useful. Was the shuttle too old and too shaky? Were all feasible emergency provisions made? Was funding adequate? Have manned flights been overdone, their glamour and propaganda value blinding us to practical alternatives?

Were we learning anything up there? For all the hundreds of experiments carried on by these floating, jolly travelers, "the scientific community has viewed the shuttle as a black hole for space dollars," the *Wall Street Journal* says in an article surveying prominent researchers.

At times such as this, though, thinkers are not much listened to. Debris and remains were still falling when we felt the first drops of a steady drizzle of knee-jerk calls to press on with man's (or America's) divinely ordained destiny to sail to the stars. Never mind the biblical command to care for the Earth.

My interest in the space program has not been great, but it has been emotional. My guess is that those whose interest is compelling are likewise propelled by emotion. They feel a need for something bigger than their individual lives and bigger than other nations can muster, and they will mourn and move on. They will forget they have left this polluted, bomb-pocked vale of tears with housecleaning undone. They put me in mind of the politically incorrect words of Edward Abbey, the southwestern novelist and wilderness defender: "Some among us have the nerve, the insolence, the brass, the gall to whine about the limitations of our earthbound fate and yearn for some more perfect world beyond the sky. We are none of us good enough for the world we have."

Stalking the Mythic Hoosier

MAY 9, 2004

Indiana government may have had its share of problems in recent years, but there seems little chance the incumbent governor will suffer for it now that he has told the voters he is both a Hoosier and a former prisoner of war.

I mean, what's a billion-dollar deficit or a few state agency scandals next to certifiable roots and 1970s reminiscences, right?

Joe Kernan has been to hell and back. Mitch Daniels has only been to Washington and back. Close does not count.

Ah, but Mitch not only has great big deficits of his own to boast about. He has roots of his own in our herbicide-enriched soil. Like Kernan's, they're not native, but like Kernan's, they are deep. And if he's going to have a shot at the chief executive who got shot down over Vietnam, he will have to plow that ground.

Schlepping around in an RV and chatting up old guys in hybrid corn caps will not get it done. Even people who say "schlepping" know that. The Hoosier who's Hoosier enough to win this race will be the one who shows us who's the Hoosier once and for all.

He not only will visit every small town in the state, but he will also make it a policy to avoid being seen in or near urban areas at all. This will serve to distance him from Kernan, who grew up in South Bend, a metropolis far, far too large to be compatible with Hoosier values. The fact the candidate himself is from Indianapolis will have to be dealt with through tearful renunciation, much in the manner of youthful marijuana experimentation.

The checks that come from Indianapolis or Fort Wayne or New York City to cover the small-town candidate's campaign expenses can be sent via bonded courier, or, when the eminence of the donor requires, begged for in back seats of limousines parked discreetly near airport runways. But public appearances in cities or suburbs will be avoided, inasmuch as we all know true Hoosiers reside in tiny hamlets with high school fieldhouses along two-lane blacktop roads. Who can hope to win without that bloc?

Likewise important: vocabulary. A candidate's positions on education issues may strike a chord with a voter here and there, but let him misidentify crick as "creek," spatial as "special," or pert nigh as "approximately," and he's exposed as a pointy-head. Everybody knows a Hoosier would not abandon the mother tongue that served our mumaws so well. No college talk or East Coast accents around these parts. May as well expect to hear Spanish.

That is not to imply the candidate should ignore the ethnic diversity of the electorate. At Red Men's lodges and Eastern Star temples throughout the state, politically active folks are serving up Spanish rice and Chef Boy-Ar-Dee spaghetti, chicken chow mein, and Aunt Jemima pancakes. It takes an international menu to become a national leader in obesity, and a prospective state leader will clean his plate and say uh-huh to seconds. Joggers and vegetarians can look in California for government work.

Finally, the true Hoosier candidate will not prance about dressed in a suit and necktie unless he currently earns his living as a funeral director. The uniform of the day for the honest neighbor who just up and ran for governor because he figured it was time your voice got heard in Indinnap-liss remains open windbreaker and button-down shirt, jeans optional in factories and Red Wings (scuffed) mandatory in hog confinements.

All set? Godspeed, Bud. Don't forget to pack your King James and your Kin Hubbard.

Reagan's American Picture
JUNE 9, 2004

Rarely has a president succeeded in personalizing the office as Ronald Reagan did. Rarely has there been a wider gap between person and persona.

A twice-married movie actor who was not all that close to his children, he was held up by his admirers as a champion of those family values Hollywood supposedly seeks to undermine.

A nonchurchgoer, he was venerated by those religious conservatives who despised the Southern Baptist Democrat who later occupied the White House.

Unabashedly attracted to wealth, power, and pomp, he came across as a Dutch uncle to the common people whose services he cut, a union man even as he crushed a federal union.

Safe in Burbank during World War II, he enjoyed a he-man image while his vice president and onetime rival, a combat veteran, was caricatured as the sissy.

Though he presided over unprecedented deficits, a deep recession, Faustian foreign entanglements, and a staff from which more than a hundred departed under clouds of corruption, he left a name synonymous with successful conservatism in many minds.

Reagan was, like his movies and his apocryphal anecdotes and his "defeat of communism," never quite real.

And yet his impact on the country was very real indeed. Today, his shadow looms like an implacable god over every officeholder and office seeker who considers espousing ideas that might get him tagged a liberal.

The influence and esteem commanded by this mellow, smiling delegator owes itself to his vision for America, if you ask his partisans, and to his exploitation of divisions over that vision, according to those on the other side of the social, racial, and ideological divide.

What neither camp cares to make much of is Reagan's signature gift, which combined both the Hollywood his admirers distrust and the savoir-faire his detractors will not credit. For lack of a better word, call it presence.

Shortly after his book *Dutch* was published in 1999, biographer Edmund Morris told me he considered Reagan a great president largely because of his "command of theater," the lack of which made his more intellectual predecessor Jimmy Carter ineffective on the global stage. At home, Reagan's crowd appeal was even more formidable.

In his 1987 book *Reagan's America: Innocents at Home*, historian Garry Wills ascribes to this president a keen sense of where the American majority was—not necessarily in reality but in self-perception.

The young Reagan spent time as a Chicago Cubs radio broadcaster, following the common practice of taking the play by play of road games by teletype in the studio back home and narrating as if the action were in front of him. The audience was not fooled; it wanted to believe. The same principle worked on a far grander scale in the movies, with their tidy America of white picket fences and red-blooded, Red-routing heroes. Even young people in the 1980s yearned to live that myth; they were ripe for a leader who would affirm it, and Reagan—"the ideal past, the successful present, the hopeful future all in one"—aimed to please. "If, to recognize that miracle, one must reject historical record for historical fantasy, fact for parable," Wills wryly wrote, "it is a small price to pay."

As we lay to rest one of our most revered and reviled presidents, that cinematic aura around him and around ourselves will live on—far from all embracing, but, like the fictitious dying words of Ronald Reagan's George Gipp, all-American.

Fathers Playing Catch
MARCH 27, 1996

Sometimes when all else fails, when ennui and frustration have built to the breaking point and the whole world feels like a conspiracy, March raps on the door bearing warmth and baseball, not necessarily in that order.

I have been rescued by the Elysian game more times than I could possibly count, perhaps as often as I have been stabbed by it. Beauty and serenity carry the price of competition, and sooner or later our teams, and our kids' teams, will pay that one with a mouthful of dust.

Brick dust is about the best, they tell me. Tons of orange building material pulverized to piles of fine slivers, used as infield dirt for its sure-bounce smoothness and its absorption ability in the event of rain. My son has been trudging home with the evil rouge caked to his pants and his cleats nearly half his fourteen years on Earth.

It slices clothing, this stuff; mothers, if I might be permitted a stereotype, feel that should override its value to shortstops charging grounders. If sports is indeed to teach life lessons, then they've got a point; let the bad hops come, and learn from them.

Let the dads roll and rake the infield all week long; let the kids lurch to the plate burdened by helmets and face guards and even cushioned vests; there's still no failing to learn baseball's lesson that loveliness hurts. That vindictive little missile has left the imprint of its stitches on my son's arm (nice job; take your base), has scratched the retina of his eye (infinite are the roads leading to the emergency room), and left welts on his ego (changeup, strike three called).

Such is the cost for the young, who would call themselves shortstops, pitchers, hitters, and for the not-young, who would be saved from some of their weariness and real-life losses by baseball. Breaking through the stony ground in spring and throwing color into the cold is painful, hazardous and, to those who have the germ within them, irresistible.

This season, I'm thinking about a fellow named Bill Warren, who died last August in Florida, where he enjoyed a busy retirement.

In Indianapolis, Bill had been a lot of things, including city police and fire commissioner, Democratic Party big shot, and board member of the Indianapolis Indians. Most poetically, he had been a part-time big-league baseball scout.

More than a decade ago, I stood alongside him at a high school diamond in Noblesville, taking notes as he sized up a slick little shortstop whose special skill landed him a college athletic scholarship and a professional contract. The old scout took as much pleasure in the nonchalant warmups as in the tense swooping and firing the kid did in combat. "He just looks like a ballplayer," Bill exclaimed, and at that moment neither of us cared who was president of the United States, when nuclear weapons would be abolished, or why the guy next door made more money.

This season, as I think of Bill and other kindred souls who require no justification for their anachronistic passion, I have my daughter as an addition to the lineup. She is six, she has got her aluminum tee-ball bat and her new Kirby Puckett autograph Wilson glove, and she has a tendency to swing with her hands apart, as the great Ty Cobb did, but should not have.

Whether she will stick with the game after taking a few on the arms and shins, like her brother, I will not chauvinistically speculate. I am aware that she and I on a gray blustery March afternoon—she laughing as I press the soft ball against my face (eye on the ball) before lobbing it to her—form a tableau for people driving by, and they smile, and all us older ones sense the returning without end, good as new, amen.

Winning, Losing, Surviving
NOVEMBER 2008

For my generation, the two Grant Parks in Chicago, 1968 and 2008, constitute a set of political history bookends. Or perhaps twin peaks.

On the one hand, street protest has yet to regain the height of participation and intensity reached in the days of the 1968 Democratic National Convention. Nor did those zealots dream that the mainstream process that had so alienated them would produce an African American president, well funded and bourgeois friendly, forty years thence.

I have known people who knew Grant Park 1968 very well. Enough years have passed that some were not around to share Grant Park 2008, that incredible scene of joy and conciliation, after wandering with me so long in the wilderness of Nixon-Reagan-Bush.

It may have been the last election this old guy will care about. It delivered a winner less progressive and more moneyed than I would have preferred, but one I could nevertheless back heart and soul for his earnest and redemptive drive, his priceless symbolism. Yet when that blue flood finally broke over the parched landscape the night of November 4, I found myself more wistful than jubilant.

As he acknowledged, Barack Obama was left with a mountain of a mess; it may prove immovable. Even beyond my limited hopes for his stewardship of our dying empire, however, there was a shadow of personal loss over his triumph.

Where was Dave, where was Greg, where was Lynn, where were all the comrades who should have lived, or should have stayed in my orbit, long enough to see Chicago reborn from the ashes of incinerated hope?

Over the years, over beers, Greg would regale us about that night in Grant Park when some stranger pulled him away just in time to escape raging cops who responded to rowdy protesters with an indiscriminant assault of tear gas, clubs, and boots. As that civil war consumed its victims outside the convention, an administration presiding over a foreign war that wasted more than two million lives was reaffirmed. That regime would lose to Richard Nixon, who would continue both the war in Indochina and the war at home, and establish a political climate hostile to peace activists and cities alike.

Now, for the first time in my life and nearly the nation's, a great northern city has sent a son to the White House. Opposition efforts to "implicate" him with the 1960s peace movement fell dead, pretty much from old age. My antiwar friend Greg, who went on to become a tourism entrepreneur with MBA sons, would have laughed with pleasure. But he did not make it. Two years younger than I, he died of cancer a few months before the election night that would properly have put us both in front of the big screen at some bar, hoisting pitchers of beer.

Today, as I celebrate (well, observe), another significant birthday, I give thanks for what I have lived to see and celebrate the gift of those whose humor, wisdom, and charity carried me through the worst of times. Each of us now living will forever remember where we were when Obama graced Grant Park. Some of us have a haunted memory of that place as well, but a memory filled with grace of its own.

Letter to the Amen Corner Man

SEPTEMBER 14, 2008

Dear Lynn,

Yeah, I'm still here, five years and change since I wrote you last and—here is the real trip—twenty years after my only national political convention.

You know I could not let this occasion pass without marking an absolute career moment, one I shared so often with you it became a reflex, like a secret handshake.

Jesse Jackson's speech to the 1988 Democratic National Convention in Atlanta, nexus of the Old South, New South, and newly solid Republican South. Atlanta, where "Dr. Martin Luther King Jr. lies only a few miles from us tonight."

Eulogy fell more lightly on me then. I was just pushing forty, nearly the exact age Martin was when he was killed. I was four years younger than you would be in 2002, when a heart attack ended an incandescent life that had gone dark a year before from a knife attack on Indianapolis's streets. Lynn D. Ford, colleague, R&B freak, Christian, voice of joy, silenced.

I stoop a bit to carry these losses nowadays. They slow my rising even to cheer Barack Obama, whom you would love. They temper my anger and anguish over the bad news of the day, because I have seen it all pass just as I've borne the passing of so many who once joined me in making life and death of this ephemeral stuff. I have come to pay less attention to great events of history than I do to moments of grace.

Jesse's speech was both of those, and how we savored it. How we laughed, trading those lines. It was, we knew, a kind of African American schmaltz, a quixotic appeal to sweep away differences—"left wing, right wing," "lions and lambs"—and knit an America cozy as Grandmamma's patchwork quilt. But it was more real than realpolitik to me. I was in that press of humanity on the convention floor when those irresistible preacherly rhythms rolled out those ideals; I saw the tears streaming down the faces of black folks living beyond their dreams: "Most poor people are not lazy. They are not black. They are not brown. They are mostly white and female and young. But whether white, black or brown, a hungry baby's belly turned inside out is the same color—color it pain; color it hurt; color it agony."

Jesse was sending out echoes of Ralph "Invisible Man" Ellison's axiom, that to be American is to be black, in the sense of having the blues in your bones. You sang it as a columnist for this white newspaper. I had learned it as an apprentice for a black newspaper. Ours was a duet for the dying, courtesy of a political performer with undeniable baggage who nevertheless had the charisma to tap our deepest wells of crazy hope: "They work hard every day. I know. I live amongst them. I'm one of them. I know they work. I'm a witness. They catch the early bus. They work every day. They raise other people's children. They work every day."

Remember that, Bishop Ford? "They catch the early bus. They work every day." Poetry that could redeem a nation. Or at least change a life. Every hard day of this election, when a dream you did not dare dream heads toward realization or wreckage, I will be hearing it and you will be here.

Keep hope alive,
Reverend Carpenter

For the Governor's 2000 Letter Project
MARCH 7, 1999

Dear Indiana Inhabitant of the Third Millennium:

If I were a coal miner or ditch digger like my Irish immigrant grandparents in turn-of-the-century southern Indiana, I would feel, I suspect, something like I feel now: aching shoulders, back, and wrists from repetitive hunched labor. Sore and weakened eyes from prolonged exposure to bad light. Fatigue and frustration at the end of the workday, compensated for by a grim pride in doing what it takes to feed one's kids.

So much for the Computer Age, when leisure and creativity were supposed to replace sweat as information replaced ore.

Perhaps, wherever and whenever you're reading this in the imminent millennium, the promise of applied science will have been fulfilled at last, and you're disporting in the gentle hum of an electronic Eden.

Or, as we so wittily put it in the 1990s, not.

My bet is you have got your literal or figurative shoulder to the wheel of the latest wage-driven technology, and your children are parading off to the piper's notes of a still newer one.

In the words of the greatest Hoosier writer of our age, the fractured futurist Kurt Vonnegut Jr., so it goes. Earthlings have taken crack after unsuccessful crack at beating nature's game, and I doubt you will get it done either, even if you live to be a thousand, which you well may. But the human yearning for a perfect world will never cease, and neither will the miracles produced by our restless striving.

The other day, I delighted my eight year old and my sixteen year old by plugging us into the Internet, still a revolutionary phenomenon here in the late twentieth century. Hearing the scritch and gurgle of that Macintosh computer, watching the beady green flashing lights of the modem as they combine to link an Indiana household with the (more or less) entire world is still an awesome experience for me.

The children, like you, no doubt, are eager enough but scarcely awed. Already to them, summoning the sum of knowledge or thereabouts through a nine-inch viewing screen is pretty mundane.

Already, the kids are impatient with the slowness of the process of gathering, unfolding, and displaying the bright cartoon quilts of text, pictures, and logos that answer to the click of the ever-ready mouse. (Are these terms long since archaic to you?)

I am impatient also, but the source is different from theirs. My son may be intrigued by the possibility of conjuring real golf clubs from a tiny picture of same, but I chafe at the constant advertisements and opportunities for instantaneous push-button purchasing. It is a sales medium, as that miracle of fifty years ago—television—turned out to be, for all the democratic educational potential once claimed for it.

OK, so they have to pay the bills by deepening our consumer debt, and I have to hide my credit cards from my dependents. Notwithstanding those realities, if you look and listen for the real stuff, the Internet is a treasure trove beyond Ali Baba's dreams, if not Einstein's. Within reach of my machine are 960,912 pages containing the word "encyclopedia."

Odds are, of course, that none of the various encyclopedias will be dialed up as often on a given day as the Spice Girls (a British organization you may have covered in history class, like the Beatles). Alas, we have, through the Internet and other media, too much information, too much useless information, and too much misuse and disuse and abuse of our genius.

In a society built on free flow of ideas, legislators are struggling to figure out what to do about people who sell dirty pictures to kids through cyberspace, who threaten and terrify innocent users of the network, and skilled "hackers" who can connect themselves to business and military computer systems and wreak havoc.

As you know, human-made miracles are never free. Indeed, many would say that, given costs versus benefits, most miracles do not yield net (pardon the pun) gain. The automobile, for instance, has made my Indiana what it is, but it also breaks us every day, whether it's running us over or just running us around.

The car-free Amishman, who travels and works much like the peasant of a thousand years ago, continues to prosper in Indiana and is an icon of vitality to his neighbors with his black buggies and immense hand-built barns. He is probably still around where you are (maybe the only food grower with good soil left) and he is probably low tech, as his religion requires.

But his religion does not forbid any and all adaptation to "progress" and, heck, he may well be on the Internet, while the rest of you are marching off and singing to Lord knows what shinier wonder.

Good luck. Be happy, with and in spite of all your improvements. And be sure to take care of your back. It's the same one my grandfather had in 1900 AD and Jesus had in the year 1, and it probably has to last you a lot longer.